The Owl Among Colophons

The Owl Among Colophons

Henry Holt as Publisher and Editor

By Charles A. Madison

Holt, Rinehart and Winston
New York   Chicago   San Francisco

**To the memory of Robert Frost,
who considered himself "Holt's oldest employee"**

Contents

Preface / ix

I. Early Beginnings / 3

II. Holt's Two Significant Series / 14

III. The Courtesy Principle in Practice / 21

IV. Holt as Editor and Publisher / 28

V. Holt's Relations with James / 44

VI. Holt's Failures with Popular Authors / 67

VII. Holt's English Agents / 83

VIII. Holt's Activities in the 1900's / 98

IX. Henry Holt and Alfred Harcourt / 111

X. A Transitional Period: 1919–1926 / 128

XI. Holt's Periodical Publications / 143

XII. Holt's Own Writings / 152

XIII. Holt Relations with Robert Frost / 165

Appendix—Outstanding Holt Books / 186

Index / 195

Preface

In the New York Times *"Book Review" of October 27, 1946, Professor*
Howard Mumford Jones stated in a review of Roger Burlingame's Of
Making Many Books, *which celebrated the centenary of Charles Scrib-*
ner's Sons:

> *Books about publishers are usually among the more unrewarding*
> *parts of literature. Sometimes these volumes are products of retired edi-*
> *tors far sunk in gentlemanly anecdotage. Sometimes such a book is a*
> *piece of self-glorification issued at a centenary of a famous house, per-*
> *fect in typography and empty of critical content.*

Being a retired editor and writing to honor the centenary "of a famous
house," I have been acutely sensible of Professor Jones's strictures. Striv-
ing to avoid "gentlemanly anecdotage," I have sought to depict Henry
Holt's career as a publisher with the calm objectivity of the cultural histo-
rian. To this end I have gone over the files of the Holt firm at the Prince-
ton University Library and in the company's warehouse, Henry Holt's
own writings as well as The Unpopular Review, *and the files of* Publishers'
Weekly. *The early history of the company is based on the written record*
plus my own association with the house for over forty years. If, on the
whole, Henry Holt emerges in a favorable light, it is because I have found
him embodying the publishing industry's highest ideals and traditions.
The first sixty years of Henry Holt and Company reflected the princi-
ples and predilections of its founder, who had vainly sought to make pub-
lishing a profession rather than a business. Henry Holt fully dominated
the firm's activities and policies, insisting on the high standards and quali-
tative scholarship which have always been associated with the Holt reputa-
tion. When the house became a public corporation in 1928, it ceased being
the shadow of one man and began to take on the image of current business

x   *enterprise. Weathering the severe depression of the 1930's, greatly bene-
fiting from the boom of the war years in the 1940's, the corporation began
to expand under the present management until it became one of the largest
all-around firms in the publishing industry. Respecting the wish of President A. C. Edwards, who wanted this volume to be primarily a tribute to
Henry Holt, I have limited this history of the company to 1928. I have,
however, included a chapter on Robert Frost's relationship with the firm,
which began in 1915 and ended with his death in 1962, since he was the
distinguished literary link between the old company and the present corporation and an author who made publishing a glorious experience.*

*If publishing has not been, at least until recently, highly rewarding fi-
nancially, it has been one of the most dignified and gratifying pursuits—
truly "an occupation for gentlemen." One of the delightful by-products of
publishing is warm friendships with authors. Holt's intimacy with many
of his "clients" yielded him vastly more satisfaction than his considerable
financial gain. I have therefore related at some length his relationships
with William James, Henry Adams, and other prominent authors, as well
as Robert Frost's dealings with his several Holt editors, climaxed by his
intimacy with A. C. Edwards.*

*I take this occasion to express my gratitude to everyone who has helped
me in connection with my work on the book. I am particularly thankful to
the officers and staff of R. R. Bowker Company and to the directors and
their associates of the manuscript divisions of the Princeton University Library and the Houghton Library at Harvard University. Helen D. Eder-
sheim read most of the manuscript and has saved me from numerous stylistic infelicities, and my wife, Edith H. Madison, has been most painstak-
ing in her perusal of the manuscript, so that her emendations are to be
found on nearly every page; to both I am deeply indebted.   —C. A. M.*

The Owl Among Colophons

I. Early Beginnings

Henry Holt was the first important publisher to begin his career after the Civil War. He came of an old Connecticut family, but was born in Baltimore on January 3, 1840, where his father had established himself in the oyster business. When six years old, Henry was sent to General Russell's school in New Haven, where he remained until he was ready to enter Yale College with the class of 1861. Bright and avid for knowledge, Henry did well enough to win a prize in Greek at the age of eleven; but the strict discipline and puritanic rigidity of the school atmosphere greatly irritated him. When only ten years old, he rebelled against the Westminster Catechism and soon developed into a religious skeptic.

At Yale, he was increasingly annoyed by compulsory chapel attendance—twice on weekdays and thrice on Sundays—and "by the puritanical mistrust of anything that had an element of pleasure in it." He was one of the half-dozen students who were not converted during a religious revival that took place in his freshman year. Instead, he and Edward Rowland Sill, the future poet, agreed "that whatever is is wrong. . . . We despised and hated the dogmas around us, and were sadly put to it to find faith in anything."

Holt's intellectual restiveness caused him to neglect his studies and he failed of promotion in his sophomore year. The shock of this setback caused him to concentrate on his courses and he soon rose to near the top of his class. In his senior year he won the Yale literary medal. He was also elected the class poet, and his long valedictory poem was both felicitously phrased and philosophically solemn. His failure of election to Skull and Bones was a traumatic experience and incited his hatred of the "sham secrecy" of college societies.

Holt wanted to devote himself to writing, but he feared the precariousness of authorship. He therefore enrolled in the Columbia Law School,

4   from which he graduated in 1864. The year before chance had caused him to join George Palmer Putnam in issuing a sumptuously illustrated edition of Irving's THE SKETCH BOOK, which appeared in time for the Christmas, 1863, season and proved a mildly profitable venture. Holt also bought a third interest in THE REBELLION RECORD, edited by Frank Moore; but with Putnam preoccupied as a Federal tax collector and with Holt taking a cavalier attitude toward the project, the work suffered from inattention and was sold in 1864 to David Van Nostrand. George Haven Putnam thus characterized his father's youthful partner:

> Young Holt had business ambition and a full measure of business capacity. He appeared, however, not prepared to believe in those earlier years that business success called for persistent application. I find that quite a proportion of his business correspondence during the first year as a publisher was conducted from Kittatinny House and from other pleasant hotel resorts. He was then, as he has since remained, a man of most winning personality, and a loyal friend, with a keen sense of humor and large individual force. He possessed decided views on a number of questions, and possessed, also, an unwillingness, possibly an exaggerated unwillingness, to accept traditional beliefs or the conclusions arrived at by previous generations. His sturdy independence and straightforwardness of character made him, in spite of an occasional perverseness, a very valuable ally and associate.

Having the year previously married Mary Florence West, Holt found that his "patrimony was not quite equal to matrimony." While waiting in his law office for clients that never materialized, he translated About's THE MAN WITH THE BROKEN EAR. Concurrently he received "another blessing in disguise: for it sent me to work like a tiger." The death of his father in a railroad accident in 1853 had provided him with a considerable inheritance. Tempted to place a large part of it in speculative Pennsylvania oil stock, he soon lost the money he had put into the venture. Now in genuine need of earning a living, he turned to publishing as the next best thing to writing. Remembering well the dictum of Yale librarian Daniel Coit Gilman: "If you find on a book the imprint of Ticknor and Fields it is probably a good book," Holt hoped to emulate this famous house in his own career.

In November, 1865, he called on Frederick Leypoldt, a minor publisher of good reputation, to interest him in his About translation. Leypoldt offered to bring out the novel at Holt's expense, which the latter refused. Leypoldt, however, was favorably impressed with the young man and offered him employment as his assistant. Holt immediately accepted. Putnam, informed by Holt of this job, wrote the following letter of recommendation on November 19, 1865:

Learning from my esteemed friend Mr. Henry Holt that he had some conversation with you in regard to business arrangements,—it gives me much pleasure to say (although I am personally unknown to you) that my relations with Mr. Holt have been of the most agreeable and satisfactory character—that I consider him a gentleman of high character and ability—a man of honor and integrity—"whose word is his bond"—and that his talents for business as well as his literary ability and his education, render him a desirable and reliable associate.

As implied in the letter, talk of a partnership was discussed from the outset. On January 1, 1866, the firm of Leypoldt and Holt was a reality.

6 Holt invested most of his remaining capital, $6,000, as his share—only to find that Leypoldt's assets in the firm were a debit of $11,000.

Frederick Leypoldt was born in Germany in November, 1835, and migrated to New York twenty years later, where he became a clerk in F. W. Christern's bookstore. After four years of service, Christern helped him open a store of his own in Philadelphia. He specialized in German and French importations and became the American agent for the Tauschnitz editions of British authors, for Firmin Didot's books, and for Trübner of London. A lover of books and music, Leypoldt made his shop a rendezvous for the city's literati and musicians.

When the duty on books during the Civil War was increased from 7 to 25 per cent and had to be paid in gold that had tripled in value, Leypoldt's business dropped precipitously. In 1863, he began to publish his own books, bringing out English translations of Andersen's THE ICE MAIDEN, Liszt's LIFE OF CHOPIN, Mendelssohn's LETTERS FROM ITALY AND SWITZERLAND, Heine's BOOK OF SONGS, and other works of high merit. James T. Fields, on a visit to Philadelphia, sought Leypoldt out and said, "I especially hunted you up to make your acquaintance, for I was curious to see the man who ventured to publish books that older and richer houses would be afraid of." Leypoldt also published foreign-language texts, edited by the best available American scholars in conjunction with Christern in New York and S. R. Urbino in Boston. In 1864, he moved to New York.

Leypoldt and Holt were exclusively publishers, being the first who did not also operate a bookstore or a printing plant. Both men were of one mind in their desire to provide American readers with good translations of the best European writers, very much like B. W. Huebsch and Alfred and Blanche Knopf a half-century later. The first joint publication of Leypoldt and Holt was Eichendorff's MEMOIRS OF A GOOD-

FOR-NOTHING. Other early publications on their list, in addition to
Leypoldt's backlog, were books by Maurice de Guerin, Octave Feuillet,
Théophile Gautier, George Sand, Ivan Turgenev, Heinrich Heine, Johann
Schiller, and uniform editions of Thackeray and Kingsley. In 1867, Holt
added his own translation of About's THE MAN WITH THE BROKEN
EAR with the following dedication to Leypoldt:

> You have not forgotten that nearly two years ago, before our busi-
> ness connection was thought of, this identical translation was "re-
> spectfully declined" by you with that same courtesy, the exercise of
> which in frequent similar cases, each one of us tries so hard to shove
> on the other's shoulders. I hope that your surprise on reading this
> note of dedication will not interfere with your forgiving the pertinac-
> ity with which, through it, I still strive to make the book *yours*.

Subsequently Holt also translated and published About's THE
NOTARY'S NOSE. This he dedicated to his able stenographer to whom
he had dictated the translation in the midst of his business involvements.

At first none of the firm's miscellaneous books sold well enough to
yield a profit; it was only the income from importations and foreign-
language textbooks that kept the partners financially solvent. In the
1870's, an article on the firm in the New York EVENING POST stated
that as late as 1868 Holt was so discouraged that he contemplated seeking a career in some other business. That year, however, sales improved.
Thereafter profits rose annually until the panic of 1873. "It is cause for
satisfaction," the EVENING POST writer continued, "to know that a
house founded on correct principles has had such an experience."

In 1870, Holt was informed by Urbino, with whom he was closely associated, that illness was compelling him to sell his list of foreign-lan-

8 guage texts. His price was $10,000 cash plus half of the gross profits on his books for the first two years; royalties on copyrighted texts would, of course, have to be paid to the authors. After some bargaining, Holt bought the list, thereby temporarily overextending the firm's credit. The list was a good one, however, containing such popular texts as Otto's French and German grammars and Cnore's Italian grammar. Holt also bought the plates of the foreign-language books published by De Vries, Ibarra and Company, another Boston firm.

An innovation made by Holt was to ask teachers using the firm's books to send him errors found in them, as well as suggestions for their improvement. Corrections and emendations were then made with each new printing. As a result, Holt texts were among the most widely used and were adopted almost exclusively in such high-level institutions as Harvard and Yale. In 1872, Holt proudly announced in the WEEKLY TRADE CIRCULAR that his firm published "more than twice as many works as any other House in America, presenting a variety suitable to the wants of Instructors from the nursery Governess to the university professor."

During this period Holt "worked like a tiger." He was quick to master publishing procedures and practices, and his fertile mind and high ideals readily made him stand out among his peers in the industry. An instance of his enterprise may be seen in the following letter to Harriet Beecher Stowe in August, 1868: "Dear Madam, We learn through Mr. Kinney that you have not yet selected a publisher for your new novel. Please get the highest offer you can, add to it five per cent and consider the sum your offer." On the same day he wrote to her sister Catherine to ask about her book on housekeeping: "If you have not yet engaged a publisher, will you be kind enough to tell us whether you would care to place it in our hands, if you would give us some idea of its scope and size and of your ideas regarding its pecuniary value to you?"

His share of work increased as Leypoldt's interest veered toward the bibliographical and functional aspects of publishing. In 1868, Leypoldt transformed the circular promoting the firm's books into the monthly LITERARY BULLETIN AND TRADE CIRCULAR, which recorded among other items the publications of American and foreign books. It was his ambition to make it a general periodical for the industry, and this aim was finally achieved with the purchase in January, 1872, of George F. Childs' AMERICAN LITERARY GAZETTE AND PUBLISHERS' CIRCULAR. This periodical he combined with his own to form PUB-LISHERS' WEEKLY. With the Publishers' Board of Trade making the magazine its standard and official organ, Leypoldt stated that "as a guide to booksellers and book buyers it is almost infallible, and has no equal." To avoid suspicion of partiality he had previously sold his share of the partnership to Holt and had moved to separate quarters. The separation was friendly and Holt declared that "no man deserved more credit for elevating the character of the book trade in this country than Frederick Leypoldt."

In 1871, Holt took in as a partner Ralph O. Williams, a Yale class-mate, and the firm's name was altered accordingly. Two years later Williams decided to leave publishing for the more lucrative field of banking and the firm assumed the name of Henry Holt and Company.

The firm's textbooks continued to be the profitable part of the business. Its two French grammars—one written by Leypoldt years earlier under the anagrammatic pseudonym of L. Pylodet—sold between 2,000 and 3,000 copies a year. Professor W. D. Whitney's GERMAN GRAMMAR and COMPLETE READER averaged a sale of 2,500 copies each over the first six years. Otto's grammars did much better, selling around 6,000 annually. Numerous other texts added to the firm's gross profit.

Holt's prime interest, however, was in the "miscellaneous" or trade

10 list. Ideas excited him; good writing aroused his admiration. Herbert
Spencer's philosophy became immeasurably the strongest influence upon
his active and searching mind. He wrote later: "About 1865 I got hold
of a copy of Spencer's FIRST PRINCIPLES, and had my eyes opened
to a new heaven and a new earth. . . . Spencer taught me that, roughly
speaking, what is, is the best possible at the moment, and can be made
better only by Evolution, which can be promoted by gradual and experimental supercession, but not by blind destruction." In time Holt became
fast friends with such admirers of Spencer as John Fiske, William
Graham Sumner, and E. L. Godkin. The latter, spokesman for many
American intellectuals in his capacity as editor of THE NATION, Holt
considered his "chief adviser" and consulted him frequently about authors and manuscripts.

Holt's devotion to Spencerian principles was not only steadfast but
salient, affecting his thinking throughout his life. In 1880, when Professor William Graham Sumner was in imminent danger of dismissal
from his chair at Yale because of his insistence on teaching Spencer's
philosophy in his classroom, Holt wrote to him:

> I am glad the issue has come. If theological tests are to be applied
> to untheological subjects at Yale, it is time the facts were clearly
> published. . . . Of course you will stick to your position. If you leave
> your chair, you can, if you care to, draw the same income from me
> that you now draw from the college, if you will give me the same
> time that you give it, and you need not change your residence.

Peacemakers, however, effected a compromise between President Noah
Porter and Professor Sumner, and the latter continued to teach in his
alma mater to the end of his career. Why he later gave his magnum opus,

FOLKWAYS, to Ginn rather than to Holt, the latter could never fathom.

Remembering Gilman's dictum about Ticknor and Fields, Holt wanted his books, bearing Leypoldt's original owl imprint, to be generally accepted as works of "intrinsic worth." Yet he definitely did not care merely to reprint works by English authors, as was then the common practice; especially so after 1870 when he heard Frederick Macmillan refer derisively to American publishers as "simply reprinters." In his determination to bring out meritorious books of his own choosing, he limited himself to those he liked personally. As he wrote to one author in 1878: "Our policy is the sad one for publishers, of not issuing anything we don't believe in." Among his early publications were Turgenev's FATHERS AND SONS in 1867 and the Russian's other books in the ensuing years, the entire writings of Hippolyte A. Taine, Bjornson's THE FISHER MAIDEN, John Fiske's TOBACCO AND ALCOHOL, Raphael Pumpelly's ACROSS AMERICA AND ASIA, Thomas Hardy's early novels, E. B. Tylor's PRIMITIVE CULTURE, J. S. Mill's AUTO-BIOGRAPHY and later his miscellaneous works in a uniform edition, Henry S. Maine's ANCIENT LAW, William Graham Sumner's HISTORY OF AMERICAN CURRENCY, and Lewis H. Morgan's ANCIENT SOCIETY. Though none of these books sold particularly well, their "intrinsic worth" was obvious to all.

An instance of Holt's mettle while still financially insecure was his decision to bring out Taine's HISTORY OF ENGLISH LITERATURE, a massive work, even after the English publisher who had issued Taine's earlier books had refused to take even a share of the risk. Holt also doubted the profitability of the project, but thought too highly of the author not to undertake it. In 1871, he published the translated manuscript in two volumes. To his pleasurable surprise the work became his "first important business success," selling around 7,000 sets in three years and remaining an active item in various editions to the end of the century. Taine was so pleased to receive royalties from America on a book he could not copyright that he paid Holt the compliment of letting him arrange for both the American and British editions of his FRENCH REVOLUTION. In 1873, Holt issued his A TOUR THROUGH THE PYRENEES, illustrated by Gustave Doré. PUBLISHERS' WEEKLY called it "one of the most exquisite specimens of American bookmaking." Issued as a gift book for the Christmas trade, the book sold well at $10.00 a copy. In 1875, Holt brought out a handsome uniform edition of Taine's writings in twelve volumes.

An admirer of Mill, Holt was eager to bring out a uniform edition of his works. Since they were on the lists of several publishers, he offered to buy the plates. Unable to obtain LOGIC and POLITICAL ECONOMY, he published Mill's other writings in thirteen volumes. More attractive than the English edition, it enabled Mill to receive greater recognition in the United States than in Great Britain.

Holt was at this time at the height of his imaginative enterprise. A news item in PUBLISHERS' WEEKLY of November 21, 1874, reported that he had in preparation "a library of biography in 12-mo volumes, to be devoted respectively to great statesmen, soldiers, painters, sculptors, philosophers, poets, historians, preachers, lawyers, doctors, etc. Each volume will be under competent editorship, and will present an outline history of the arts which its subject practiced. The style and arrangement will make them equally useful to the instructor and general reader." Another venture was a series of Condensed Classics, edited by Rossiter Johnson. Holt's idea was to give readers of current novels a chance to familiarize themselves with the essential parts of older novels in the least amount of time. "The aim has been to cut out everything that a skillful novel reader would skip, and everything he might skip if he

knew what was coming. This condensation leaves the novels, on the
average, almost half of their original bulk." Among the first novels condensed were IVANHOE, OUR MUTUAL FRIEND, and THE LAST
DAYS OF POMPEII.

Selling books by subscription was at that time a common method
among publishers, and Holt began doing so in 1876. His first work
was AN ABRIDGMENT OF THE DEBATES OF CONGRESS FOR
1874–5. To obtain agents, the firm advertised for "gentlemen" able to
bring the book to the attention of every public official and lawyer in
the United States. These agents received 40 per cent of the list price
as their commission. Some of the other subscription books issued by
Holt were Goodholme's DOMESTIC CYCLOPEDIA: A FAMILY REC-
ORD, and the two-volume HISTORY OF YALE—Holt's pet project.
Charles Holt, Henry's younger brother, who had just entered the firm,
sought to increase the sale of these subscription books by offering as
much as 55 per cent to the more aggressive agents. He was particularly
proud of the DOMESTIC CYCLOPEDIA, which had taken three years
to prepare and was not "a thing flung together for an ephemeral sale,
but a good, honest work." In a letter to a prospective "hawker" he
wrote: "The names of those who have been engaged in its preparation
are a guarantee of its high class. It is concise, practical, useful, con-
venient, cheap. . . . It contains a great deal for everybody—rich or
poor, in country or city, and will yield honor and profit to the canvasser."
Although he wrote scores of letters to agents, none of the subscription
books sold well enough to encourage Holt to continue this part of the
business.

II. Holt's Two Significant Series

14 Henry Holt's two major achievements as a publisher were the Leisure Hour Series and the American Science Series. Very early in his career he conceived the idea of publishing a series of well-written novels in a suitably attractive format and at a relatively low price. In 1872, after numerous experiments with designs, he issued the first group of novels in his now-famous Leisure Hour Series: Turgenev's SMOKE and FATHERS AND SONS, About's THE MAN WITH THE BROKEN EAR, and three other novels. His first price was $1.00, soon raised to $1.25, and in 1877, with the emergence of the cheap paperbacks, reduced to $1.00. The flyleaf of each volume contained the following statement: "A collection of works whose character is light and entertaining, though not trivial. While they are handy for the pocket or the satchel, they are not, either in contents or appearance, unworthy of a place on the library shelves."

The obvious superiority of the series both in content and in format gave it high distinction among similar series issued by other publishers. In June, 1873, the New York TRIBUNE expressed the hope that it was proving profitable. "The approval of their own conscience may be enough for these meritorious publishers, but good pecuniary returns for an enterprise so praiseworthy would exercise a wholesome moral influence upon the book trade generally. They have not printed an objectionable book as yet, and not one which was not worth reading." Four years later the TRIBUNE was pleased to note that this was "one of the most popular series in the higher class of cheap literature." By that time the Turgenev novels were selling 1,000 a year each, Hardy's books had reached a maximum of 8,000, and Mrs. Alexander's WOOING O'T obtained a top sale of 20,000.

Holt continued to add to the series in the 1880's, though reluctantly, in the face of the ruinous competition of the cheap piratical reprints,

selling at 10 cents a copy. It numbered around 200 in 1890, when he
disposed of it.

Among the distinguished European and American writers included
in it were Henry Adams, Berthold Auerbach, Walter Besant, V. Cher-
buliez, Hugh Conway, Octave Feuillet, Jessie Fothergill, Gustav Freitag,
Goethe, Hardy, Heine, Fanny Kemble, W. E. Norris, J. P. F. Richter,
Shakespeare (7 volumes edited by Dyce), R. L. Stevenson, W. L. Wal-
ford, and Theodore Winthrop. A number of these writers were first
introduced to American readers in this series.

In 1883, in a vain effort to compete with the pirates, Holt had started
the Leisure Moment Series at prices ranging from 20 to 35 cents. These
paperbacks, many of them from the Leisure Hour Series, were noted
for their large type and good paper and they were sewn with thread
instead of wired. A bookseller commented in 1884: "The admirably
edited and well-made Leisure Moment Series of Messrs. Henry Holt
and Co. is, or could be, largely sold by every intelligent bookseller in
the country." After a brave effort to market this series, Holt found it
impossible to compete with the piratical reprinters and began to veer
away from foreign fiction and to concentrate on general works and
textbooks.

Holt showed even greater initiative in the development of the American Science Series. The idea probably came to him in 1872 when he
learned about Appleton's International Scientific Series initiated by E. L.
Youmans. At the time scientists in the United States and Europe were
bursting with the excitement of experimentation and controversy. The
doctrine of evolution was fought over with fanatic rancor. Youmans,
backed by the Appletons, battled for evolution, arranging to publish
works by the leading European scientists. Thoroughly in sympathy with
his views, Holt devised the plan of bringing out a series of books by

16 eminent American scholars that would present the various disciplines from the evolutionary standpoint and be adapted to class use as well as to the interested reader. Such a series, he hoped, would discuss the latest scientific developments and thus further the acceptance of the doctrine of evolution in the United States. To his surprise he found that the outstanding American scientists "thought it beneath them to write textbooks." Persistent urging and the aid of influential friends gradually enabled him to obtain the men best suited for the purpose, although he had to make a number of substitutions in the process.

The circular on the facing page, prepared in 1874 and headed "Preliminary and Confidential" to prevent the opponents of evolution from scotching the plan, outlined the scheme in detail and listed the titles and authors tentatively arranged for.

It is of interest that only three of the nine authors named in the circular actually completed their books. The final series, however, extending into the 1900's, contained 14 books, most of them in two or three different editions, by men of stellar distinction:

PHYSICS George F. Barker

PHYSICS Arthur L. Kimball

CHEMISTRY Ira Remsen

ASTRONOMY Simon Newcomb and Edward S. Holden

GEOLOGY T. C. Chamberlin and Rollin D. Salisbury

BOTANY Charles E. Bessey

ZOOLOGY A. S. Packard, Jr.

THE HUMAN BODY H. Newell Martin

PSYCHOLOGY William James

POLITICAL ECONOMY Francis A. Walker

GENERAL BIOLOGY W. T. Sedgwick and E. B. Wilson

PHYSIOGRAPHY R. D. Salisbury

PUBLIC FINANCE Henry C. Adams

ETHICS John Dewey and James H. Tufts

PRELIMINARY AND CONFIDENTIAL.

AMERICAN SCIENCE TEXT-BOOKS

FOR

HIGH SCHOOLS AND COLLEGES.

In 1874, the undersigned initiated the preparation of a Series of Science Text-Books for American High Schools and Colleges. It is hoped to begin publishing in May, 1878. The principal objects are to supply the lack—in some subjects very great, of authoritative books whose principles are, so far as practicable, illustrated by familiar American facts, and also to supply the other lack that the advance of Science perennially creates, of text-books which at least do not contradict the latest generalizations. Especially is it intended to supply books in accordance with the doctrine of Evolution.

The prejudices against that doctrine have not, however, been forgotten, and therefore no general advertisement of the conformity of the series with it is to be made.

The following were the intentions regarding details :

Each volume to be 12mo, about 500 pages, page to contain about 400 words, volumes therefore to contain about 200,000 words, not varying more than 20 per cent. in either direction. Space taken by illustrations, to be computed as if by words.

The teaching, as far as practicable, to proceed from facts to principles. Verbal illustrations, especially from American facts and experiences, to be used very freely, and pictorial ones as much as really desirable, though not for the sake of mere elaboration.

As far as practicable, the authors to compare notes so as to secure mutual conformity and support, and exclude duplication.

As each volume appears, the authors of the others to avail themselves of anything it may suggest toward rendering their own work a part of an organic series, instead of a disjointed treatise, and to give the authors of the published books hints for bringing subsequent editions into as close correspondence as practicable with the rest of the series.

The books thus far arranged for are as follows:

I. PHYSICS.
 By ALBERT M. MAYER, Professor in the Stevens Institute of Technology, and ARTHUR W. WRIGHT, Professor in Yale College.

II. CHEMISTRY.
 By SAMUEL W. JOHNSON, and WILLIAM G. MIXTER Professors in Yale College.

III. ASTRONOMY.
 By SIMON NEWCOMB, and EDWARD S. HOLDEN, Professors in the United States Naval Observatory.

IV. GEOLOGY.
 By RAPHAEL PUMPELLY, late Professor in Harvard University.

V. BOTANY.
 By GEORGE L. GOODALE, Professor in Harvard University.

VI. ZOÖLOGY,
 By A. S. PACKARD JR., Professor in the Salem Institute, and Editor of the *American Naturalist.*

VII. THE HUMAN BODY.

VIII. PSYCHOLOGY.
 By JOHN FISKE, late Lecturer on Philosophy in Harvard University.

IX. POLITICAL ECONOMY.
 By FRANCIS A. WALKER, Professor in Yale College.

X. GOVERNMENT.
 By EDWIN L. GODKIN, Editor of *The Nation.*

HENRY HOLT & CO., PUBLISHERS,
25 BOND STREET, NEW YORK.

E. L. Godkin was one of the first to be approached, and he agreed to write the book on government. Holt kept prodding him, gently yet persistently, keeping him informed of the progress made by the other contributors and reiterating the importance of his book to the series. He also consulted him on problems arising in connection with the project. In November, 1879, to give him more time, he wrote to explain that the series "has a certain integral system and completeness regardless of the order of publication. . . . It is inconvenient and unnecessary to wait until the authors should all be ready to publish in the order of the scheme." Yet Godkin never did write the book. His transfer from THE NATION to the EVENING POST not only deprived him of the needed time but also unfitted him, as he later stated, for concentrated writing.

Simon Newcomb, noted economist, mathematician, and astronomer, agreed to write the volume on ASTRONOMY in collaboration with E. L. Holden of the United States Naval Observatory. In their correspondence Holt encouraged Newcomb to discuss the nebular hypothesis "but not preach it loudly or hotly." He further intimated that he did not want anything said that would prevent readers from putting "a God behind any law that science announces." He also urged Professor Holden to try out the manuscript in the classroom. "There," he explained, "will come the crucial test of the circulation of the books, not in the opinion of the learned."

ASTRONOMY, the first volume in the series, was issued in 1879 and its general excellence and favorable reception established the high level and usefulness of the series. How careful Holt was about its utility is seen in his comment in 1881 to Holden, who was preparing the AS-TRONOMY: BRIEFER EDITION, "It should have mighty little about instruments, as the pupils using it will never see an instrument. It should consist almost entirely of *results; processes* are for the specialist."

In 1876, Godkin suggested General Francis A. Walker, then president of Massachusetts Institute of Technology, for the volume on POLITICAL ECONOMY. Walker agreed to do it. Six years later he sent Holt the first part of the completed manuscript, which he jocosely called a "famous, illustrious and widely circulated treatise on Pol. Econ. by a writer at present but little known." In fact the book quickly occupied a commanding position in the field of economics. In 1884, Walker's POLITICAL ECONOMY: BRIEFER COURSE came out and was found in certain areas an improvement on the larger book. It was equally well received in England.

After failing to persuade Dr. S. Weir Mitchell to write the volume on THE HUMAN BODY, Holt wrote to his old friend D. C. Gilman, in 1878 president of Johns Hopkins University, to tell him about the series and to express the wish that Gilman would persuade H. Newell Martin, professor of biology and formerly Thomas Huxley's collaborator, to prepare the book. "Your register doesn't show anything nearer to it than your Prof. of Biology; but the subject appears near enough to his line. What is wanted, is just what ALL your students ought to know before being old enough to graduate, and I'm sure he could tell them that."

Martin accepted the task, and his book became the most successful and longest-lived volume in the series. Holt, the practical publisher, made sure that the work contained nothing that would be found objectionable by the conservative teacher. In writing to Martin about the inclusion of the subjects of coition and orgasm, he advised him also on other controversial topics: "It might be just as well to omit from your very neat peroration the suggestion that persons of authority enough to justify your allusion doubt the existence of any life after this. Of course, I

20 doubt it myself, but that doubt doesn't help the sale of school books."

To keep the series going, Holt had to exercise great patience, constant concern, and adroit diplomacy. Professor G. E. Goodale of Harvard appeared to be making good progress on the botany book, and even tried parts of it out in his classroom; in the end he found himself unable to complete it. Holt had to turn quickly to Professor Charles E. Bessey of Iowa State University, his next choice, and the latter wrote a text that remained a standard work for many years.

For several years Holt prodded Professor S. W. Johnson of Yale to write the volume on CHEMISTRY. Early in 1878, informing him of the progress of the other contributors, Holt remarked jestingly, but not without asperity, "Lord what a job it is to get you wise men to work and to keep you at it." When Johnson also failed him, he was fortunate enough to interest Professor Ira Remsen of Johns Hopkins in the book—in the end a happier selection. When his first choice for the PHYSICS fell through, Holt signed up Professor George F. Barker; when the latter was slow in producing the work and Holt learned that Professor Arthur L. Kimball of Amherst was writing such a book, he quickly offered him a contract—and in time published both texts in the series. Only many years later did he find the right authors for the GEOLOGY, PHYSIOGRAPHY, and ETHICS. Holt's efforts in connection with William James's PRINCIPLES OF PSYCHOLOGY are treated in Chapter V.

III. The Courtesy Principle in Practice

The "courtesy of the trade" principle came into fairly wide acceptance some years prior to the Civil War as a means of eliminating cutthroat competition. It assumed that the publisher who first announced his interest in a foreign book had priority to it; to establish this priority he had to possess a copy of the work. Violation of this principle was frowned upon by reputable publishers.

In his eagerness to further the professional character of publishing, Holt sought to establish the "courtesy" principle on an industry-wide basis. With no copyright on foreign books, he believed that only by such means as "courtesy" could publishing be kept from chaotic competition. Regular publishers professed to practice it, but some of them occasionally took unfair advantage of it. Some announced books which they happened to hear about but were not at all certain they wanted. The result was often confusion and caustic correspondence. Because Holt adhered to the spirit as well as the letter of the "courtesy" principle, he insisted on his rights when they appeared to be violated. He and his able assistant, Joseph Vogelius, who had come to Leypoldt as a boy shortly before Holt and who remained with the firm as its most trusted associate till 1919, watched every publisher's announcement of a forthcoming book and were quick to act in instances where their own announcement had priority. The following sampling of citations of such occurrences indicates the extent to which the Holt firm went in promoting the "courtesy" principle, mostly successfully.

In July, 1868, Holt wrote to the publisher, G. W. Carleton, to ask him to desist from publishing Renan's ST. PAUL, since "some time ago, Mr. Renan invited us to publish a translation being made by a friend of his under his own eye." Two months later he wrote to Harper concerning a novel announced by both firms: "As we understand the usages of the trade, we are under no obligation to stop, but we don't feel big

22 enough to fight you if you see fit to act on a different opinion." In
November, he wrote to Little and Gay of Boston that neither they nor
Roberts Brothers had any right to Auerbach's novels, as the Holt firm
had for some time been his authorized publisher. "We are satisfied that
we have the right on our side and that we can issue an edition early
enough to make opposition futile." Concurrently he informed both Appleton and Lippincott that his announcement of Mendelssohn's REMI-
NISCENCES had appeared prior to theirs.

Late in 1868, Holt consulted Putnam regarding a book which Harper
had announced without having a copy, while he—though still feeling too
weak to battle with so large a firm—did have a copy. Six months later,
however, he wrote to Harper to complain, diplomatically, against their
publishing an edition of one of his books. "The justice and courtesy
you have always manifested toward us, prevent our believing that you
have undertaken thus to run us opposition, without some reason that,
to your minds at least, justifies it. We depend upon a continuance of
that same justice and courtesy to lead you to tell us what the reason is.
If we have violated any trade propriety, we want to know it." Several
days later he again wrote to Harper that, since as many copies of the
novel in dispute could be sold at 75 cents as at 40 cents, "why should
not our edition be sold and both firms reap the benefit?" In May, 1870,
when Harper announced its intention to issue Taine's INTELLIGENCE,
Holt wrote to ask, "Doesn't the fact that we have published several of
his books entitle us to that if we want it? We are not sure that we do,
but it's best to be clear on the point." Harper acquiesced.

In October, 1872, Holt wrote to both Harper and Lippincott that his
announcement of Mrs. Craven's FLEURANGE preceded theirs by six
weeks. "We have the story all translated. Trusting you will withdraw in
our favor . . ." They did. Early the following January, Holt told Lip-

pincott that in announcing a new book by Gustav Freitag "we take it for
granted that our announcement escaped your attention." A year later
he again wrote to Lippincott concerning another German importation:

> We have not intended to play dog-in-the-manger regarding Werner.
> We have kept him in reserve to fill a gap with. You certainly have
> some rights as a pioneer, however, and we will either make up your
> losses and take your plates, or withdraw all our announcements (in-
> cluding GOOD LUCK and wishing it to you) in your favor. We
> would rather pay a good price for your plates, though, and try him
> in the Leisure Hour Series.

In September, 1872, Vogelius wrote to Lippincott to explain that Holt
had contracted to publish Mrs. Paar's new book without knowing that
any other American publisher had any exclusive rights to her work; that
in view of the need of this book for the Leisure Hour Series, he hoped
Lippincott would permit Holt to proceed. He also wrote to Harper that
their announcement of WOOING O'T, already plated by Holt, violated
the "courtesy" principle.

In February, 1873, Holt told Harper, "we have been indebted to you
for so many acts of courtesy" that he wondered about their announcement of Hardy's A PAIR OF BLUE EYES. "The book is by the author
of UNDER THE GREENWOOD TREE, which we have now in press,
or rather in the stereotyper's hands. If our little venture proves it worth
anybody's while to print BLUE EYES, oughtn't we to have the chance?"
He got it. Appleton had also announced the novel and likewise desisted.
In April, Holt asked Scribner to withdraw from publishing Lord Houghton's MONOGRAPHS in view of his earlier announcement. Scribner
also complied.

24   In January, 1874, Holt wrote to A. K. Loring, a small publisher, concerning his edition of WHICH SHALL IT BE?

It would have surprised us under any circumstances that you should publish without consulting us a work by an author whose reputation we have made. That you should publish such a work after our announcement of it passes our understanding altogether. Your refraining from making any announcement previous to your own publication adds to the negligence of the proceeding. Will you favor us with an explanation?

Loring admitted his error and asked to be "forgiven." Holt insisted, however, that he had to publish his own edition of the novel to protect himself in the trade. He therefore proposed that Loring send him the "plates and stock with a statement of outlays and receipts"; he would dispose of them as seemed best, and would credit Loring with half of the profits till his deficit was made up. Holt was firm in his insistence on some such arrangement. "We can't retire at all as long as you are in the field; though we hate bloodshed as badly as you."

When James R. Osgood proceeded in 1874 to publish Hardy's FAR FROM THE MADDING CROWD without knowing that he was trespassing on Holt's preserves, the latter—realizing that Osgood had acted honorably under the circumstances—volunteered to assume the amount already spent on the plates. That December, Holt wrote to Harper: "We notice your announcement of PATRICIA CAMPBELL. We are now considering the advanced sheets. If we want them, we suppose you'll give us free swing?" They did.

In June, 1875, Vogelius wrote to Lippincott and to Appleton to point out that Holt's announcement of THE HAND OF ETHELBERT had preceded theirs. "We of course claim Hardy as our man as we have introduced him to the American public and when we add that we have published all his works by direct arrangement with the author, we trust that you will withdraw in our favor." They did.

After making several other protestations in the course of the next two years, Holt was similarly called upon by Lippincott to desist. Charles Holt promptly replied that they had not noticed the announcement but "that your having called our attention to the matter is sufficient to cause us to withdraw at once." A month later Holt again withdrew in favor of Lippincott when the latter established the fact that it had an advance copy of a certain book before Holt had.

Holt continued to press the "courtesy" principle upon the major publishers, who acted upon it in almost every instance. In writing to Scribner concerning Symonds' STUDIES AND SKETCHES IN ITALY, Holt said: "We've been lately fatuous enough to start a printer on his RENAISSANCE IN ITALY. Don't you think that after we've taken that risk on him you'd better leave us the field to make something out of it if we can?" Scribner agreed.

The character of publishing insofar as it involved uncopyrighted books began to change radically with the emergence of the cheap "libraries," which included everything potentially salable. The piratical publishers completely ignored the "courtesy" principle and in time brought the fiction market to a condition of chaos. Rejecting a novel by Mrs. B. H. Buxton in 1879, Holt wrote to her: "Within a year or two past, there have sprung up here a number of unscrupulous reprinters of all successful stories; who pay authors nothing and publish in cheap pamphlets without covers. Their proceedings have led to quite a general abandonment by the regular houses of fiction which our defective laws do not protect."

26   These pirates took popular nonfiction as well. John W. Lovell, for instance, issued a cheap reprint of Taine's ENGLISH LITERATURE, ruining the sale of Holt's regular edition. Seaside Library managed to bring out a cheap edition of Auerbach's BRIGITTA before Holt could bind his, thereby greatly curtailing the sale of the authorized edition. The pirates brought out cheap editions of Stevenson's NEW ARABIAN NIGHTS and other Holt books that had a popular appeal. In 1883, Holt wrote to William Blackwood and Sons in Great Britain:

> You can have no idea of the glut of fiction in this market. Within two days after publishing ALTEORA PETS, should we do so, there will probably be at least three editions of it on the market at a merely nominal price. One of them will be our own made from plates that we use for our ordinary cloth issues. We send you a couple of specimens of that edition. We publish it only for the sake of forcing the price of a rival edition below the profit level. We see no immediate prospect of any profits from it to ourselves.

To the English publisher, George Bentley, with whom he had a close association, Holt complained: "No self-respecting publisher can run a series very successfully in America against the pirates who will take every book that comes, no matter what the publisher's claim upon it may be." In rejecting T. Fisher Unwin's English offerings, he wrote: "We regret we cannot use them, as we have concluded, under ordinary circumstances, to use no more non-copyrighted matter." In 1884, he told an English author that "the breakdown in the old usages of the American publishing trade, which acted to some extent as substitutes for an international copyright law, has so far destroyed the market for books such as you have done us the honor to submit, that we find ourselves unable to undertake it." And throughout the 1880's, Holt published very few books that he could not copyright.

IV. Holt as Editor and Publisher

28 Imaginative and idealistic, if also practical, as Holt was as a publisher, he was at his best as an editor. Although he usually had readers' reports on manuscripts before he read them himself, he perused those he wanted to publish and his pencil noted freely the suggestions and emendations that occurred to him. He knew intuitively as well as from hard experience what was likely to make a book successful, and he gave each author the benefit of his editorial judgment. His approach to authors is best exemplified in his relation with Professor Packard while he was writing ZOOLOGY for the American Science Series. In April, 1876, Holt wrote to ask him how he was progressing with the writing and continued:

I've just received from Eaton the botanist—an old friend of mine, but not a book-maker—a sentence which seems to me so suggestive of the sort of book that our series requires, in every department, that I am moved to copy it for you.

"What I would wish for your series is that someone would make an abridgment of Sachs' work, and also give a popular treatise on *all* the natural orders of plants, of the whole world, giving some little popular account of all useful plants—as the fruits, grains, fiber-plants, tea, coffee, chocolate, indigo, chicoria, poppy, vine tobacco, nutmeg, camphor, aloes, oaks, pines, fancy woods, &c."

Mutatis Mutandis, it seems to me that that's just the sort of a book that we need in zoology.

Holt prodded Packard several times with no results. Two and a half years later Packard sent him a specimen chapter. Holt read it with his usual incisiveness, and his comments contain such excellent editorial criticism and guidance that the long letter is given in full:

Smile your broadest and get yourself into the most amiable state of mind you can, for I'm going to be disagreeable.

I. What have I ever done to you that you should give me such a looking piece of MS. to read? It takes double time, and makes it impossible for the thought to enter the reader's mind without being all ground up and patched together again.

II. What have you done to yourself that you should be willing to have your work judged from such distorted and mutilated presentations of it? Not even your *alter ego* could get it in such shape and do it any sort of justice.

III. A chapter out of the middle of an organically constructed book is, at best, a hard one to take as a sample. Its relations with what goes before are too essential a part of it. So far as it is practicable to judge from any single chapter, the first one is the best. There is everything in the way a subject is opened up. Newcomb sent me, a year or two ago, the opening chapter—showing the scheme of presentation of his astronomy. I pulled it all to pieces. He rewrote it and rearranged his scheme to fit my ignorance, and therefore, the ignorance of those his book is to teach.

It is very seldom that a man who is really full of a subject can put himself in the place of a person approaching it. The perspectives of the two men are the reverse of each other. A string of facts which are to the writer full of significance and connotations, to the learner often have no significance at all, and might as well be a string of words in an unknown language for all the nutriment his mind gets from them. Especially is this apt to be the case if the ignoramus takes up the subject after it is started, as I did the chapter you sent. If the learner is supposed to have been taught a good deal of zoology in the earlier part of the book, that chapter may not go in one ear and go out at the other; though it has a good deal of that effect on me, and I believe I know more about the general outlines of Biology than the average student will be apt to before he passes that stage in the book.

I've peppered the chapter with comments very unreservedly, and I have faith that you will take them very amiably. I've generally put a red mark near them to call attention to them.

I find what I probably told you that I expected to find: that you need to assiduously cultivate ignorance in order to do this book well. I presume you selected this chapter to send me on the conviction that if I passed it without criticism, I would pass anything else in the book. If I were to judge from it, you have started to make your book contain about four times as many facts as the mind for which it is intended can assimilate, and not over one-fourth the exposition and little sentences by way of guide-lines and reminders that such minds need. You're not supposed to be writing a book for working zoologists, or even working students in zoology. When you write a book for them, you've got to put into it more than 500 twelvemo pages and get for it more than $2.00 or $2.50. You can, of course, write a book in those limits that would be of great use to the working student, but it would have to presuppose much that it is the function of the present book to teach. This book is intended not for a laboratory or seacoast directory, but to bring a student from nowhere to the point where he could *begin* to use such a directory intelligently.

For the sake of crowding in your facts—many of which have no significance to the student using his first book, you use a condensed and technical style of expression that presupposes considerable familiarity with the subject. You prefer a technical word where a common one will answer the common student's purpose, sometimes for the sake of giving an exactness which the common student can't appreciate, or, as already intimated, for the sake of getting space to dire him with still another fact that he hasn't the training to assimilate.

Now my feeling about this might be somewhat different if I had read from the beginning of the book up to the part which you sent me, and so approached technical expression by easier stages; but if, as I presume, this chapter belongs pretty near the beginning, the steps to it must, at best, be pretty high and steep for the learner.

Remember you are not writing for even your NATURALIST reader, but for readers whom you wish to train to read the NATU-RALIST.

Illustrations and details of my points (I submit "details of a point" is a good metaphor) you will find penciled on the chapter I express back.

Do you know that we can get the Dana cuts called for in this chapter?

Before you send me any more MS., possess your soul with mercy for me and the printer and wherever a page is very bad, have it copied off. Some of the pages look very fair, but, at best, your hand is nearly as bad as mine.

Henry Holt's strength as a publisher was his ability to meet authors on their own intellectual level and give them the benefit of his intuitive and incisive editorial sagacity. His lofty ideals combined with a relentless forthrightness to irritate many an author, as he did William James; but nearly all, James included, admired his keen intelligence and devotion to principle, and many became his intimate friends. Holt warmly reciprocated this friendship, on a basis of full equality, for he had a high opinion of himself. An active member of the leading New York clubs—a founder of Yale, City, and University clubs and prominent in the Century Club—he associated freely with the leading men of his time. A

32   sense of pride stopped him from taking professional advantage of these associations; indeed, his strict adherence to the "courtesy" principle kept him from taking on published authors who would have been glad to be placed on his list. Nor would he, in the 1890's, meet the unreasonable royalties and unjustified advances offered by other publishers to his popular authors—losing them as a consequence. The following discussion of his relations with several important writers indicates the close association that often develops between an interested publisher and his leading authors.

In 1873, Holt was the first to issue a novel by Thomas Hardy under his own name. This was UNDER THE GREENWOOD TREE. Hardy's first six novels were in the Leisure Hour Series by 1878, and four additional ones appeared in it subsequently. Holt dealt directly with Hardy and paid him the usual royalty. As a matter of courtesy he helped to place Hardy's writings with American periodicals. In 1874, he sent Hardy a copy of SCRIBNER'S MONTHLY, which contained a favorable review of FAR FROM THE MADDING CROWD, and informed him that "its publishers are desirous of securing a story from you. When you are ready, I will act as your intermediary, if you care to have me." A little later he wrote him about a misunderstanding with Osgood concerning FAR FROM THE MADDING CROWD but that he was "satisfied that all the apparent contradictions were natural" and that Osgood would "turn the publication in book form over to us with the best of feeling." In July, Holt sent him "an additional remittance of £50, which it gives me great pleasure to do so." He then asked for the remainder of FAR FROM THE MADDING CROWD in order to take advantage of the summer market.

In December, 1875, Holt, proud and principled, acknowledged a misunderstanding of a recent letter from Hardy. "I confess that I did feel

seriously hurt at your appearing to think it advisable to impose conditions on me regarding your next book. Your letter sets it all right and
makes me regret having fallen into the mistake." He added that since
English publishers remitted royalties only once a year, he would do
likewise with British authors. "If, however, you are strongly disposed to
urge a semi-annual settlement, I will hereafter return to the old method
in your case." Several months later, when Hardy complained about the
delay in royalty payments, Holt was quick to speak his mind. "I am now
going to take the liberty of asserting that you have been better treated
by me than happens once in fifty times when a British author's book is
reprinted in America, and of expressing, among the many good wishes
that I entertain toward you, that you may hereafter be more thoroughly
conscious of similar facts."

In 1878, HARPER'S MAGAZINE was serializing THE RETURN OF
THE NATIVE and Holt was co-operating with the editor by arranging
the publication of the novel about the time of the final installment. The
following year Holt visited England and met Hardy. On his return he
wrote him: "I seize a moment to add the expression of my regards and
to say that the idea of our charging you a commission for placing your
book with a periodical is not to be thought of." Shortly thereafter Holt
sent him a draft amounting to $500 which DEMOREST'S MAGAZINE
paid for serializing THE TRUMPET MAJOR.

With the rise of piratical reprinters the sale of Hardy's books, till then
moderately good, dropped precipitously. Nevertheless Holt continued to
publish his novels. Early in 1880, he learned that Harper had bought
both the serial and book rights to Hardy's forthcoming book. He immediately called on Joseph W. Harper, then the senior partner, and told
him that trade "courtesy" required that he turn the book rights over to
him on the basis of his usual arrangements with Hardy. After some dis-

34 cussion Harper "ended up by doing exactly what I wanted, and what the notions of honor then prevalent among publishers of standing required. . . . Subsequently, by an amicable arrangement, Harper took over certain relations with Hardy, yielding to me in return similar relations with Norris."

At that time Holt thought more highly of W. E. Norris than he did of Hardy. Nor was he alone in considering the quality of Norris' fiction as approaching that of Thackeray's novels. In 1881, he was pleased to publish Norris' MATRIMONY along with Hardy's A LAODOCIAN. A cheap reprint of Norris' novel cut deeply into the sale of the regular edition, but Holt told Norris that "the praise of the discriminating" has assured the literary success of the book. "Personally," he added, "I must allow myself the pleasure of thanking you for the pleasantest hours I have spent over a novel in many years." When, months later, Norris said Holt could have all his work, Holt replied, "Nothing of the kind could be more agreeable to me than your inclination that I should have the refusal of your books in the future. Though they are not the most remunerative that I publish, there are none that I am gladder to publish."

In 1882, Holt issued Hardy's TWO ON A TOWER and four years later THE MAYOR OF CASTERBRIDGE. Although the fiction market had been taken over by the pirates, Holt assured Hardy that "we will do the best we can with it in these distressing times when it seems next to impossible to do anything with anything." Hardy, however, thought that Holt was not doing enough for him and went over to Harper. In 1890, having disposed of the two Leisure series, Holt sent Hardy his final royalties. By way of explanation he told him that heretofore he had refused to sell the series to pirates in order to protect the authors in them, but recently the pirates had begun paying for advanced sheets and were thus enticing a number of these authors. "Now that our authors have

begun voluntarily placing themselves in those hands, the only question
for us to consider is the only one they have appeared to consider—the
amount of cash offered. . . . We might say much regarding the probable
result of this state of affairs, and as to whose advantage it will ultimately
inure, but it may be wiser to leave all that to time to show."

Holt published ten of Norris' novels. Notwithstanding their modest
sale and their increasingly critical reception, Holt's loyalty did not
slacken, although his admiration had definitely abated. Late in 1889,
however, when Norris informed Holt about a tempting offer he had received from one of the pirates, the response was nothing if not candid:

> If I knew who made you the offer you quote, I might be able to tell
> you "something to your advantage." . . . I may as well tell you in a
> general way that some of the pirates who have destroyed the American
> book trade and wiped out the profits of British authors for ten years
> past, have now, through a paradoxical process . . . got to the point
> where they can sometimes outbid the publishers who have given
> British authors virtually all they have hitherto had from this market.
> They do not make a habit of paying, but they pay occasionally for a
> variety of reasons. They do, however, make a habit of failing, however
> magnificent may be the promises they fail on.

By 1890, Holt had ceased publishing both Hardy and Norris.

When Lewis H. Morgan submitted his manuscript of THE ANCIENT
SOCIETY to Holt, neither the author nor the publisher had any idea
that the book was to achieve the high prestige it did. Holt liked the work
but was doubtful of its market and asked Morgan to share with him the
risk of publication and receive double royalty, to which he agreed. Mis-

36 understandings as to details—one entailed a charge of $12.00 for proof-reading—soon arose and their correspondence only generated disagreement. Holt, frank yet friendly, wrote to Morgan in November, 1876:

> I'm sorry we could not discuss the points that have been at issue, by word of mouth. I think I talk as much better than I write as you seem to think I write better than I print, and I know that I like to hear you talk much better than I like to read your letters. You write as if you had some pretty tough experience with publishers and had come to believe them all sons of Belial; but when you were here you bore yourself as if you would not deny the possibility of salvation to the humblest of them.

After THE ANCIENT SOCIETY was published, its very favorable reception quickly established it as a work of prime anthropological importance. Henry Adams, then at Harvard, wrote to Morgan that the book "must be the foundation of all future work in American historical science." Morgan was anxious to have the book issued in England, and Holt submitted it to John Murray with a letter extolling Morgan's fine reputation in Europe, but Murray saw no market for it. Macmillan finally bought sheets, which yielded little to either Morgan or Holt. In reply to further bickering by Morgan on matters that were normally routine procedure, Holt wrote to him in May, 1878:

> You're one of toughest men to correspond with and one of the pleasantest men to talk with that I ever came across.
> Now let's drop the discussion until we can talk it over. I'd give up the trifle involved five times over rather than try to settle the question by correspondence.

Perhaps you'll be edified to know that it is with Whitney just as it is
with you. When we talk, things settle themselves at once: the more we
write, the more they get mixed. All of which goes to show that great
scholars should visit their publishers oftener.

Holt's relations with John Addington Symonds were ideal. After reading THE HISTORY OF THE ITALIAN RENAISSANCE, Holt wrote
to him in February, 1879:

My reading of it has inspired me to send it to the printer. But because business is very dull and because among us now the nearest approach to an active taste is in the Fine Arts, I have thought it best to
begin with the volume on them, and I have felt justified in doing so
by the considerations stated in the enclosed memorandum for a
Publisher's Note. . . . Hoping that my efforts (which I do not claim
to be disinterested) may give your noble work the circulation here that
it deserves, I am dear sir . . .

Holt printed an edition of 500 copies of the Fine Arts volume, but its
sale was very slow. Despite this poor showing he was ready to bring out
the other volumes of THE ITALIAN RENAISSANCE and urged Symonds to provide the duplicate plates of the English edition. Two years
later he published THE AGE OF DESPOTS and THE REVIVAL OF
LEARNING. Soon after their appearance Holt informed Symonds: "It
gives me great pleasure to tell you that the publication of them has re-
vived interest in the volume we first published, and that the enterprise
will be remunerative." In the following year he sent Symonds a draft
for £20 "as a very modest 'first fruits' of the publication of the REN-
AISSANCE in America." Later still Holt brought out the volume on

ITALIAN LITERATURE. The entire set was promoted vigorously and sold fairly well over the years—though not as well as the high reputation the work would indicate.

Holt maintained a wide acquaintance with both civic leaders and outstanding writers and scholars. Among his friends, in addition to those who were his authors and advisers, were E. C. Stedman, Charles Dudley Warner, John Hay, Clarence King, and Henry Adams. To them he was not merely an eminent publisher but a congenial companion and their peer intellectually. Because he almost never used his friendships to solicit manuscripts, his intimates misunderstood his professional pride and seldom offered him their books. Henry Adams, for instance, though an admirer of Holt, went to other publishers with his historical and biographical writings. It was only when he wanted to bring out his novel in strict anonymity that he turned to Holt.

In 1879, Adams sent Holt the manuscript of DEMOCRACY "under a pledge of dead secrecy." Holt accepted it at once—especially since Adams insisted on paying the cost of publication. To Holt's credit it must be stated that the identity of the author remained undisclosed until it was revealed in 1915 in a biography of John Hay.

In March, 1880, a "Literary Note" in the New York TRIBUNE announced: "The Leisure Hour Series is to have added to it the first novel by an American author. Its scene is laid in New York and Washington, and its author would appear to be a resident of one place or the other. It is intimated that many readers will imagine they see portraits in the book." A second printing was ordered a month after publication; but the sale of the novel was relatively slow.

The English edition, highly praised by Gladstone, became popular in that country. News of this popularity stimulated readership in the United States. In September, 1882, Adams wrote to Holt:

"Dear Pirate:

"The time has come when I want to make a twenty-five cent edition of the scandalous libel. If there is no profit in it to you, there ought to be glory." He added that the accumulated royalties would cover the possible loss. In a later letter Adams said, "Announce as much as you please that a twenty-five cent edition is coming out or is out; but don't spend your money on advertising opinions of the press."

When the cheap edition appeared and Adams received a copy, he thanked Holt for the trouble and added, "The truth is, I was afraid the little bastard was fairly becoming British, and my parental heart could not stand such a perversion of nature." He then offered to pay the costs of the unsold copies of the regular edition.

In November, 1885, Holt, unaware of Adams' distress on account of his wife's mental depression, suggested that DEMOCRACY receive fresh promotion. Adams replied: "By-gones are pretty well by-gones, and I am not so particular as I was; but, all the same, I am peculiarly anxious not to wake up the critics just now. . . . I never had so many reasons for wishing to be left in peace, as now." In time the novel went through a total of twenty printings, the 1925 edition being issued under Adams' name and with a preface by Henry Holt, and with the latest printing in 1952. To his brother Brooks, Adams gloated: "The wholesale piracy of DEMOCRACY was the single real triumph of my life."

In 1884, Holt brought out Adams' ESTHER as the third volume in the American Novel Series under the pseudonym of Frances Snow Compton. Adams insisted that review copies were not to be sent out nor was the book to be announced in an advertisement. When Holt remonstrated, Adams explained that he wanted to wait at least two years before he considered "whooping up" the novel. Several months later he was more explicit: "The experiment I wished to try here was whether authorship

40 without advertisement was possible. I understand you agree with me that the result, as far as a single experiment can go, proves that advertisement is necessary to authorship." The total sale amounted to 514 copies of ESTHER, and years later Adams bought the remaining volumes and destroyed them.

Adams asked Holt to place ESTHER with an English publisher and permit him to send out review copies. "I want to test English criticism and see whether it amounts to more than our own. As you know, I care little for readers and dread notoriety more than dyspepsia; but I like the amusement of a literary conundrum." The English edition proved no more successful than the American.

After Mrs. Adams' suicide, ESTHER took on deeply intimate connotations to Adams. Writing to Elizabeth Cameron, one of his "nieces," after the appearance of his HISTORY OF THE UNITED STATES, he said, "I care more for one chapter, or any dozen pages of ESTHER than for the whole history, including maps and indexes; so much more indeed, that I would not let anyone read the story for fear the reader would profane it." An explanation was offered in June, 1886, by Clarence King to John Hay, members of the famous "Five of Hearts," which included Mrs. Hay and the Adamses:

[Adams wanted] to see if a dull world would do their own criticising and appreciate his work.

Later came to his mind a second reason why he should let the novel lie where it had fallen in the silent depths of American stupidity and that was the feeling of regret of having exposed his wife's religious experiences and, as it were, made of her a chemical subject *vis à vis* religion, as in DEMOCRACY he had shown her in contact with politics. Later when Dr. Hooper [his father-in-law] died of heart failure,

as the old man in ESTHER died, he felt that it was too personal and
private a book to have brought into its due prominence, so he let
it die.

In March, 1890, Adams, ready to sail to the South Seas in the hope of
forgetfulness, wrote to Holt:

With the year 1890 I shall retire from authorship. As an occupation
I can recommend it to the rich. It has cost me about a hundred
thousand dollars, I calculate, in twenty years, and has given me that
amount of amusement. In July I sail from San Francisco for new
scenes and adventures, leaving to younger and better men whatever
promotion my vacancy may cause in the service. I hope they will enjoy it as much as I have done.

Nine years later, in January, 1899, in response to Holt's inquiry about
a new work from his pen, he wrote in a similar vein—years before he
composed his two most famous books.

The only novel I care to write or read is the story of how good
people get completely out of this world into something else. You may
wipe the sponge over all I ever did, or, in other words, burn or otherwise destroy all record of it. I doubt seriously whether God Almighty,
in case he exists, will ever ask to see it, and I think I'm tolerably certain not to put it in evidence on the trial. As for literary work, I have
handed my ink-pot over to my brother Brooks, who has ten times
my intelligence, and who will say at least ten times in excess of what
I could do.

Oh, yes! I've wanted to say lots of things. But what is the use!

42   "What do they understand?" Not even their blossoming interest tables. Let me be re-born a Jew!

In April, 1907, Holt wrote to Adams to inquire if he objected to having DEMOCRACY serialized in newspapers. Adams' reply was equivocal, and Holt wrote that unless he heard from him to the contrary he would proceed with the arrangement, which he did.

Six years later, in September, 1913, Holt again wrote to Adams, this time to ask for a copy of his privately printed autobiography:

My Dear Historian:

Can you remember as far back as when you were that to me, and I was your dear philosopher to you? I remember the time so vividly that I find no difficulty in telling you that Pumpelly spoke to me the other day about your book THE EDUCATION OF HENRY ADAMS in such a way that I want you to send me a copy. . . .

Adams was then in Paris, sufficiently recovered from a stroke to be on his feet again but more mordant than ever, as is evident in his reply, quoted in full:

I was moved to a laugh when I read your letter yesterday. That three old men like Pumpelly, you and me, should go muddling about each other's forgetfulness still, after we were dead and forgotten these thousand years, seems a merry jest, but Shakespeare said something about comparing him with the bettering of the time as an excuse for such behavior in his own case, and although no one has yet found the betterment he kindly promised, no doubt everyone revels now in plenty of Shakespeares and such to encourage you to read me. Un-

luckily, I don't carry my immortal works in my pocket. I must wait
for winter, but if I survive till December I will try to find a copy of
my immortal thoughts. But pray remind me of it, for I remember
nothing over night;—least of all, about myself, which is a subject fit
only for the ghosts. Oh, yes, I like it! but I think even the ghosts are
rather bored. Well they may be!

It is no great use wishing you all the blessings of youth and love-
liness but whatever falls in your way I trust will do you good. For
my own part I want only personal beauty. It has a good influence on
my contemporaries.

After Adams' death in 1918, Holt wrote to Senator Henry Cabot
Lodge, Adams' literary executor, to suggest the idea of publishing
ESTHER on the other side of the coin—over Adams' name and giving
it full promotion—in order to see what would happen to the novel under
these contrary conditions.

Lodge replied: "ESTHER is new to me. I have never heard of it
and as I have been an intimate friend of Mr. Adams for nearly half a
century I am a little surprised that I never saw it or heard a word from
him in regard to it."

Two months later Lodge again wrote to Holt: "I know that Mr. Adams
wrote ESTHER and I know the facts as to his experiment to be as you
describe them." He stated, however, that the family felt "it would neither
be agreeable to Henry, nor would it be for his reputation, for either
DEMOCRACY or ESTHER, whatever that may be, to be republished."
That ended the matter, though in 1924 no objection was raised to Holt's
new edition of DEMOCRACY.

V. Holt's Relations with James

44 As already shown, Holt's relations with authors were not always smooth and sweet. He was too forthright and critical not to irritate the sensitive writer. Always, however, his effort was to make a good book better, and if his comments were sometimes cutting, his intent was co-operative and courteous. This attitude is best illustrated in his correspondence with William James.

When he wanted an author for the book on PSYCHOLOGY in the American Science Series, he turned to his friend John Fiske, who was the leading Spencerian in the United States and in Holt's estimation a universal genius. Fiske, however, was not able to undertake the work and in 1878 suggested James as the likeliest person for the project. Holt lost no time in writing to James, and the response was prompt and favorable. "Nothing would please me better than to do the PSY-CHOLOGY for your series of American Science books. Your proposal merely gives definiteness to an intention which I have long harbored in my mind but should probably have still longer postponed without this spur." He made clear, however, that his other engagements and his uncertain health would keep him from completing the book before the fall of 1880. Holt was "a little staggered by the length of time which you think it would take to write the PSYCHOLOGY," but nevertheless offered him a contract with the standard royalty of 10 per cent of list price.

Five months later James, now married, and all the more worried about his commitment, informed Holt that he was not certain he could finish the book on time. Holt replied that, although he did not know what to do about a book for the series, "my *impulse* is to draw on faith and hope, and wait for yours." In October, 1881, with the manu-script hardly begun, Holt, having learned that Professor G. Stanley Hall was well along on his book in psychology, asked James to "give

Prof. Hall to understand that I'm the publisher for his psychology book."
He intimated that whether or not he would put this work in the series
would depend on circumstances. Hall, however, gave his book to another
publisher. All through the 1880's sporadic letters between Holt and James
made evident the latter's throes of authorship and their growing friendship. In April, 1887, Holt eagerly accepted James's offer of intimacy:
"Certainly: 'Drop the Mister' and I'll drop the Prof. We've made one
or two spasmodic attempts in the direction before, I believe, but, much
to my regret, circumstances make our intercourse too spasmodic throughout." Holt at this time consulted him concerning a projected book on
Hume and asked if the philosopher's "reputation as an 'infidel' would
not keep him out of almost every institution but Harvard." The response
was favorable to the project.

James continued to work at his Herculean task despite the most
painful agonies of authorship. Neurasthenic, subject to psychosomatic
illness, exceptionally scrupulous, and eager to produce a work of high
merit in a discipline that was still in its infancy, he struggled with the
expression of new ideas and concepts until they emerged in his final
draft with crystal clarity. But the effort was stupendous. In 1879, he
wrote optimistically to his colleague Josiah Royce, "I am writing (very
slowly) what may become a text-book in psychology." Four years later
he complained to his French friend, M. Renouvier, that he now understood "why no really good classic manual of psychology exists. . . . It
is impossible to write one at present, so infinitely more numerous are
the difficulties of the task than the means of their solution. Every chapter
bristles with obstructions that refer one to the next ten years of work
for their investigation." To his brother Henry he wrote about the same
time: "I have made a start with my psychology which I shall work at,
temperately, through the vacation and hope to get finished a year from

46 next fall, *sans faute*." In 1887, he still hoped to "have the book finished a year from now," yet complained about the difficulties in his way. "The truth is," he told Henry, "that the 'science' is in such a confused and imperfect state that every paragraph presents some unforeseen snag, and I often spend many weeks on a point that I didn't foresee the difficulty at all." Even with the end in plain view, he still grumbled to Henry, "I have to forge every sentence in the teeth of irreducible and stubborn facts. It is like walking through the densest brush-wood."

In April, 1889, Holt reminded James that the contract made him the negotiator for the English edition and asked whether James would look for an English publisher himself or have his firm do it. Holt also told him that his new contract form contained changes that "would be for the mutual advantage" and suggested that he accept the new form. James agreed, and told Holt to seek an English publisher in his behalf. Writing again in November, Holt inquired about his health, his new house, and then added facetiously, "All these things call up a vague, though possibly mistaken, impression that you once had some idea of sending me the manuscript of a PSYCHOLOGY to publish. If you remember anything of the kind, please let me know how the matter stands."

When James was at the end of his task he became anxious to see the book in print. In January, 1890, he wrote to Holt that he would bring 350 pages of manuscript and expected composition to begin at once. Holt replied that he would be glad to see the pages, "but don't bring me anything to start making the book before you bring me the MS. complete. When you do that latter, we'll try and dispose all the orbs in the system to make the world roll smoothly." James's reaction was characteristic: "Publishers are demons, there is no doubt about it. How silly it is to fly in the face of the accumulated wisdom of mankind,

and think just because one of them appears genial socially that the
great natural law is broken and that he is also a human being in his
professional capacity. Fie upon such weakness! . . ."

Holt tried to explain why he had to have the entire manuscript before
starting composition:

> If you were gradually being converted into a demon, however,
> by the disappointments occasioned by authors, you would know all
> about it. I *never* began printing an installment of a MS., so far
> as I can remember, without having to stop work before the book
> was finished, thus forcing the printer to put away the apparatus in
> place for it, and giving him excuses (which they always avail them-
> selves of the full) for dilly-dallying with the rest of the work when
> it came, and eventually getting the work out later and after vastly
> more friction than would have been the case if it had not been begun
> till the MS. was all ready.

James came back at Holt with his irony at full blast:

> Poor publisher, poor fellow, poor human being, ex-demon! How
> those vermin of authors must have caused you to suffer in your time
> to wring from you such a tirade! Well, it has been very instructive
> to me to grasp the publisher's point of view. Your fatal error however
> has been in not perceiving that I was an entirely *different kind*
> of author from any of those you had been in the habit of meeting,
> and that *celerity,* celerity incarnate, is the motive and result of all
> my plans and deeds.

With the manuscript ten years overdue and not yet ready, Holt's
sarcasm was irrepressible and understandable:

"Celerity" is good. I don't want to throw anything in your face, but upon my soul, I don't see how, after agreeing to do a thing, a suggestion that somebody else should do it is to be accounted a valid substitute for doing it; but your sins, which are many, are forgiven, as you know. . . . And now you have the blessings necessary to keep you up to your standard of "celerity," and a few marginal ones simply as illustration of the affectionate nature of my prayers for you.

On May 7, 1890, James again began to urge Holt to start work on the design and composition of the early part of the manuscript even before its completion:

I don't see why we shouldn't be beginning already to decide on the page. The MS., to my great regret, is panning out bigger than I thought it would. I fear there will be no less than about 460,000 words, which would require 575 words on a page to make a book of 800 pp. I can't possibly cut this thing down, as it all belongs together; and I trust this bulk will not unfit it for the "Series."

In view of the fact that Holt could not well decide on the format until he was able to estimate the length of the final and complete manuscript—he later found it necessary to publish the book in two volumes—his refusal to comply was unavoidable:

I wonder what has destroyed your confidence in me! I've told you twice and given you long strings of reasons based on an experience hundreds of times as large as you can possibly have in such matters, that I am not going to set any of that book until I have it all.

You may think that if I were to turn tail and do it, you would still
have some faith in me, but you wouldn't, and I wouldn't have any
in myself.

On May 22, 1890, James delivered the completed manuscript to
Holt. Two weeks later he wrote that he felt "no further responsibility
whatever about having the thing published by October." He wanted all
proofs before September. His resentment against Holt for his refusal
to start composition sooner continued to rankle, and two days later he
gave expression to it in another letter.

When James was going over the final draft of the manuscript, he
wrote to Holt in a moment of self-abnegation:

No one could be more disgusted than I at the sight of the book.
No subject is worth being treated of in 1000 pages! Had I ten years
more, I could rewrite in 500; but as it stands it is this or nothing—
a loathsome, distended, tumified, bloated dropsical mass, testifying to
nothing but two facts: 1st, that there is no such thing as a *science*
of psychology, and 2nd, that WJ is an incapable.

Meantime the printer was setting type with all possible speed. James
wrote to his brother, "My proofs have only just begun coming in; but
they promise to come thick and fast. I take little pride or pleasure in
the accursed book, which has clung to me so long, but I shall be glad
to have it out, just to show that I *can* write a book." All summer he
sweated over the proofreading, but all went well and the two-volume
work was ready by October. The $6.00 price Holt put on it actually
came to $4.80, as it was then still the practice—resulting from prolonged
cutthroat competition—for the bookseller to give his customers a discount of 20 per cent of the established price.

On publication the book was at once hailed as an original and masterly treatment of the subject. Professor J. McKeen Catell expressed a common judgment: "It was a declaration of independence, defining the boundary lines of a new science with unapproachable genius."

Although the two-volume work was universally admired as a stellar American contribution to scholarship, it was too long and too expensive for wide class use. At Holt's urging James agreed to prepare the BRIEFFER COURSE without delay, intent as he was to earn the maximum amount out of his writing and knowing that the shorter book would sell well. By the end of July, 1891, the manuscript was ready. Although nearly half of it was new material, James described it to Holt in his usual self-deprecatory and ironic manner:

> I expect to send you within two days the MS. of my BRIEFER COURSE, boiled down to possible 400 pages. By adding some twaddle about the senses, by leaving out all the polemics and history, all bibliography and experimental details, all metaphysical subtleties and digressions, all quotations, all humor and pathos, all interest, in short, and blackening the top of all the paragraphs, I think I have produced a true pedagogic classic which will enrich both you and me, if not the student's mind. . . . The larger book seems a decided success—especially from the literary point of view. I begin to look down on Mark Twain!

Meantime James wanted an accounting on the sale of PSYCHOLOGY and Holt complied. He also told him that according to their contract James was entitled to only $14\frac{3}{10}$ cents per set of sheets sent to Eng-

land. This he considered unfair and was increasing the amount to $33\frac{1}{3}$
cents, "which I trust will be satisfactory to your temporal and spiritual
welfare."

In October, James was anxious to finish the proofreading, as he
found it "hateful to have to go so often over one's own tracks." He
also asked Holt for better terms in view of "the fact that the work
will surely be more lucrative than its predecessor," but he was ready
to settle for no charges for extra proof corrections and the preparation
of the index—"unless you have something better yet to propose." Holt
agreed to bear the extra charges, but explained that the greater cost
of promoting the text to schools and colleges precluded an increased
royalty. The book—called "Jimmy" in deference to the larger work
known as "James"—at once became the most widely used text in psychology courses over the country; selling 47,531 copies in the first ten
years as against 8,115 copies of the two-volume work in twelve years.

Holt and James were at this time close personal friends. They shared
a common interest in psychic research and frequently exchanged views
on life and philosophy in general. In May, 1893, Holt confided to
James that "having been fed on business husks most of my life, I like
to settle long enough where I could get a good fill of something solid."
Two months later he told James frankly, "I want to live better and
think better than I do, but don't see how I could get any help from
such procrastinating doctrines as you preach." Holt continued to consult him on prospective authors and books, and early in 1895 James
agreed to write a preface to the English translation of Paulsen's IN-
TRODUCTION TO PHILOSOPHY, which he had originally recommended. When Holt asked for his photograph to use in the promotion
of his books, James balked with characteristic playfulness: "I stand on
my rights as a free man. You may kill me, but you shan't publish my

52 photograph. Put a blank 'thumbnail' in its place. Very very sorry to displease a man I love so much."

For all his professed love, James never quite forgot Holt's forthright sharpness in his letters. Probably Mrs. James fanned this irritation into a growing resentment, since she believed her husband was not receiving the royalty he deserved. At any rate, he no longer thought of Holt as his exclusive publisher. Wholly unaware of this change of attitude, Holt wrote to him in September, 1895: "Haven't you got another book to put to press or can't you make one ready? I'm not the only person in the country that thinks that anything you have to say is sure to be worth saying." James did not reply till the following June, when he informed Holt that he had a volume of essays ready for publication to be called THE WILL TO BELIEVE AND OTHER ESSAYS IN POPULAR PHILOSOPHY.

A Mr. Lord from Scribner's called on me twice last winter, urging me to give him something, and that brought this long-nibbling project to a head. I don't suppose there's any money in such a volume, but I told him I would send him the MS. and then get a bid from you, and give it to the highest! Isn't that good business? . . . I also told Lord I was going to get ready for the press this summer my TALKS TO TEACHERS ON PSYCHOLOGY a very small volume. . . . N. M. Butler has also applied for them for a certain "series" he is interested in. I will here also, send them to all three of you and see if anyone promises to make me richer than the other. Wealth is now my only ideal.

Holt began his long reply—he later regretted he could not run up to

You ask me, after laying down your auction scheme, "Isn't that
good business?" No, my dear boy, it is not. It's very bad business.
The "good business" point of view for both author and publisher,
is this: When an author is identified with a house, every new book
of his gives the publisher a new chance to boom his old ones. If his
books are scattered all over creation, he loses this benefit, and it is
too important a one to lose.

Holt further explained that publishers who bid in auctions were apt
to put up the retail price to cover their bids and that tended to lessen
the sale of the book. He continued, frankly yet facetiously: "Most
publishers, like most other men, are fools; and you authors, if you
escape the fools, may be but lambs before the wolf. So your only safety
is to find as nearly a regenerate and merciful wolf as you can, and
then stick to him and let him take care of you." He further stated
that, although Scribner and Longmans were upright publishers and would
do well by him—"assuming of course that they have had as much of
a chance to learn how to love you as I have"—they were not likely to
go into auctions "to get authors away from their colleagues." As for
himself, "There's occasionally a publisher with an ambition (a perfectly
vain one perhaps) to conduct his business like a gentleman, and to receive—even perhaps by deserving—the confidence of his clients that he
will do by them as well as a reasonable and honest conduct of business
permits."

After saying that he was no longer as quixotic as he had been in
1879 when he refused to take on William's brother Henry as an

author because he "didn't want to take away Osgood's client," Holt made clear his position in regard to James's new book: "If you want to know what I would naturally do with you on these new books you speak of, I will tell you with pleasure after I have seen the copy; but I shall not on account of your auction scheme, do anything different from what I would do anyhow."

James misunderstood Holt's attitude, unaware that the "courtesy" principle was still adhered to by the more reputable publishers, and resented Holt's lofty "ideal of father and son relationship between P. and A. [publisher and author], their inseparable loyalty, and all that." It was particularly difficult for him to grasp this attitude since, as he pointed out, "Appleton, Scribner, and Longmans have all spontaneously solicited me for 'copy,' with no reference made to you. . . . Your veto on the auction business has roused in me all the freeman-blood of my ancestors, and makes it now quite impossible to publish the book with you, when before it was not only possible, but probable." Yet he ended the letter with the avowal that "as *men,* we shall love each other far more after this exchange of letters than we ever did before."

When James learned that Holt had written to Charles Scribner about the matter, he accused Holt of, in effect, forbidding "the Scribners to continue negotiating with me, and in principle confined me to the alternative of either ignoring your existence as a publisher and immediately resorting to some third house, or of passively giving you the book to deal with as you pleased." He ended by asking Holt if it would not be fair of him "to notify Scribners that the boycott has been lifted?"

Holt's patience was getting thin. He replied, "I happen to know that my effect on Scribner was precisely as imaginary as you appear to have thought it possible to be; and that his course of conduct, as carried out, was clearly decided before he had exchanged a word with me on the

subject." He then told James he would not bid on his manuscripts and
reiterated his position:

If any manuscript of yours comes here with a request to let you know what I propose to do about it, I shall let you know. What's the use of going any farther! I ought to have confined myself to that before. I don't object to telling you now, however, that my views agree entirely with yours about the reasonableness of an author's honorarium being increased after a book has paid for itself, *provided* that the book is not mainly used in classes, and so doesn't require constant attention and correspondence, and frequent extra discount for distribution and exchanges—in short it doesn't depend for a great sale more on the publisher than on the author.

Holt added that he was the first publisher voluntarily to increase royalties on a popular book from 10 to 15 per cent of the list price. He also assured him that any publisher who pushed textbooks in philosophy more energetically than he did "probably makes a nuisance of himself, and makes his circulars and letters unwelcome." In conclusion he assured him: "Well, even if you quarrel with me on such grounds as I've quoted, you do it in such a lovely way that you still keep me, affectionately yours."

Five months later, in December, 1896, James informed Holt that "the Scribner-Holt complication . . . was too deep water for me to stir up again, and as I was cut off from Scribner, I thought I would just cut myself off from you as I had previously announced." Having failed with Houghton Mifflin, he had given the book to Longmans. "As I had said before," he continued blandly, "I don't harbor a particle

56 of resentment, and when I have got ready a manuscript of TALKS TO
TEACHERS ON PSYCHOLOGY which I expect to do by next summer,
I will offer the same to you."

Their relations remained outwardly cordial. They corresponded concerning the promotion of "James" and "Jimmy." Holt consulted James
on the likelihood of John Dewey's writing an original ETHICS or making up "a book out of all that other people have seen fit to say on the
subject, whether they have really done any thinking about it or not."
James assured him that Dewey would write his own book, and on the
strength of that advice Holt asked Dewey to write the text. Holt also
inquired concerning Havelock Ellis' work on SEXUAL INVERSION
and was veered away from it.

On November 5, 1898, James informed Holt that he was sending him
the manuscript of TALKS. "What I wish is that you would kindly look
over the manuscript to gain some idea of its value, and then if you
wish it, name the most favorable contract with me which you are willing
to accord." Two weeks later, after hearing favorably from Holt, James
wrote, "I have decided that I had better manufacture the book myself
and publish it on commission. Will you take it thus, full advertising
it in your routine ways, and taking 10% of the list price for handling?
If you will, you may have the work, as I had rather you should publish
it than another."

Holt was at first nonplused by this blunt proposal, but decided to
acquiesce in it. "Have it all your own way," he wrote; "but for God's
sake, don't get stuck; for if you do, all sorts of devils—incarnate and
excarnate—will whisper to you that it was because your publishers ran no
risk of failure, and had small temptations to success, and therefore
neglected the book." He assured James that he would "treat the book
as our own," and promote it vigorously. He then pointed out that in the

case of his own book he delivered the bound volumes to the publisher,
paid for the advertising, and received half of the retail price on the
copies sold. "That's the only way I know of to publish 'on commission!' . . . You may be edified to know that your book will be the only
one (so far as I can recall) that we have on commission."

Several days later Holt wrote to explain that the TALKS "had better
be on a net teachers' price and handled like an Educational book." He
would not price it, however, "until I see the book actually in the flesh,"
since much depended on its appearance. He thought it best that they
agree on the percentage terms and proposed to give James 60 per cent of
the net price. James proved difficult at this point—mainly because he
did not understand discount terms—and Holt explained carefully what
were the customary discounts to bookstores; also the best time to publish an educational book. He further made it clear that TALKS, not being a basic text, was not the kind of work that travelers could sell in
quantity. "Our educational men are in the field till the middle of June,
and of course will do a good deal of incidental talking about the book.
But if I were to tell you that they are going to give it any special attention, I should be a fraud." Yet two days later he wrote that E. N.
Bristol, his educational manager, thought the book had a chance of class
use in normal schools "and that travelers will put in special work with
that in view."

Holt's forthright presentation of facts troubled James. Confused by
terms such as "net" and "retail," he complained:

Your epistolary manners are so rough that unless I had had already
some acquaintance with them, I should have supposed that your ef-
fusion of the first was meant as a notification that you didn't care for
the book. . . . This last letter of yours reminds me of certain other

letters I got during the PSYCHOLOGY time—well and humorously meant no doubt, but *rough!*—and I tremble at the prospect of their continuance.

Holt hastened to assure him of the contrary. "I never intended to say anything sarcastic in a letter unless I want to quarrel with a man, and I never wanted to quarrel with you. Hence if you saw anything sarcastic in any of mine, it was not there."

James, quick to anger, yet generous of spirit, readily accepted Holt's explanation:

Since you are now so sweet again let me say that the roughness in the past of which the memory haunts me was solely in the PSY-CHOLOGY days, when you playfully danced clog dances on my sensibilities. . . . Dear Holt let us both be old enough to practice in accordance with the experience of mankind, and not conduct business correspondence in sarcastic terms.

Whereupon let us be friends again—until the next encounter.

When the book was ready, James was disappointed in its appearance, since his printer had no designer and had made no effort in that direction. "We are not surprised," he was told by Holt, "that your book does not look as you expected it would. Now that you are learning the publishing business, we will impart a secret of the trade—no book ever does." Later he wrote that Ellis, the Boston printer of the volume, had made an inferior set of plates. Since the book was expected to be adopted by Reading Circles in several Middle Western states, he suggested that new plates be made in New York, to which James agreed—

admitting that "mine is the worst printed book I have ever seen of
Ellis." He was ready, he told Holt, to "leave the whole matter of size and
price henceforth absolutely in your hands. You know more about it than
I do."

At the same time he complained that he was not receiving his full
share on the state adoptions. Holt explained at length that the division
was equitable. He then made an extended personal comment on the
nature of publishing:

> I have come to the conclusion that when I declined to bid on that
> book of yours, my head was swelled—I entertained an optimistic view
> of the publishing business which the more sober judgment of my de-
> clining years does not justify. I had come to regard it as a "profes-
> sion," in which it was undignified to bid for work or seek to get it
> away from a competitor; and I had myself lived up to this standard—
> with the result (among others) I verily believe, of losing a great deal
> of business to concerns whose views were not as top-lofty as mine. I
> have come to realize, largely through the help of such concerns, that
> the "profession" idea does not hold water.

The thought that Holt was getting more than 10 per cent for his share
continued to rankle in James's mind and he complained repeatedly. With
Holt away from the office, others wrote to point out that their correspondence on the book "has been heavier than we can recall having
had regarding any other book we have published." The fact was stressed
that the firm had to go to great trouble to obtain Reading Circle adoptions and that the office expenses on TALKS must have exceeded 15 per
cent of its gross income.

60   In 1901, the Holt firm ordered a shipment of TALKS sent to its Chicago office. Ellis sent them and received a signed receipt. The New York office failed to enter the shipment in its receiving book—the letter-invoice went to the correspondence files in error—and no credit was given to James's account. When James received the bill for the shipment from Ellis without later getting royalties on it from Holt, he impulsively suspected fraudulence and wrote to Holt accordingly. Holt being in Fairholt, his home in Vermont, his brother Charles acknowledged James's complaint, expressing his shock at the oversight and offering his humble apologies. "Such errors," he explained, "could not occur with books we manufacture, as we have a long tried system of treble checks against them. In the case of the TALKS we have been without such checks, you having the only means of comparing your printer's and binder's bills with our reports of books received and accounted for. In future we shall ask Mr. Ellis for a statement each six months to compare with our entries." He enclosed a revised account and a check with interest added. In conclusion he reiterated his apologies and asked James "to be as charitable as possible." He sent James's letter and his reply to his brother.

Holt immediately wrote of his "surprise and disgust. . . . Fortunately," he continued, "the blunder is too absurd to make it possible that any thought of intention should cross a reasonable mind." He also explained the nature of the firm's bookkeeping that made the error possible. "In all this of course you won't understand me as claiming that the slip is not blameworthy, but only that it is not as blameworthy as would at first appear."

Far from allaying James's suspicion, this letter only excited his fertile and frenetic imagination to fever pitch. His prompt impulsive reply, an outburst of sheer choler, is quoted at length:

You make the whole business a more perfect abyss of unintelligi-
bility than before, by repeating what I can only call the utterly *silly*
explanation of the letter which accompanied the check.

The plain and flagrant fact is that in your last two ½ yearly accounts the *sales were falsified* to correspond to a false number
of copies received. The error was systematic. You may in explanation "change the receipt signing clerk" (*all* the receipts are by
the same hand) and "no counter-check whatever," as if your own
orders to printer, his letters of invoice, and your own sales-books
didn't exist. When you add that such an "experience was probably
bound to come sooner or later," to what sort of bookkeeping methods
do your confess!!

Am I a baby six years years old that you should write me such rub-
bish? The only impression such irrelevant explanations can *possibly* arouse is that the firm is nervously concerned to conceal something, and thinks that for a man of my lack of business experience
that kind of thing will do as a sop.

Now, my dear Holt, stand up and tell the whole truth. What, until
this last correspondence was only a puzzle, has been converted *by
your letters* in a grave suspicion of dealings which will not bear
the light. It is up to you to dispel the suspicions by something more
than what you write.

Confident that you can do so if you will, I am faithfully yours.

Holt's long reply was masterful in its restraint, in its simplicity of a
detailed account of his methods of bookkeeping, and in its dignified offer to have James come to New York at the firm's expense and see the
books for himself. He considered James's letter "the most inconsistent
human document I ever saw. It seemed to say, 'My dear Holt, I have

confidence enough in your honor to believe that you will confess your-self a damned rascal.' . . . I think it does you and me a grave injustice."

Heartily ashamed as he was of the blunder, he reiterated that accounts were not based on sales but on receipts only. "All books recorded as re-ceived which, at the time of settlement, are not on hand or recorded as given away, are accounted for as sold. This method is universal so far as I know." He stated that books received from the bindery were entered in the receiving book by clerks, but since they were not fully dependable, their checks were used "merely as an aid, to be corrected by later checks." In the case of all his books but TALKS, the firm had "bills and especially the monthly statements of the paper-makers, printers and binders." These bills appeared in conjunction for each edition, and if they didn't tally, the error was hunted up. The unfortunate expression "no check whatever" merely meant there were no bills to check against for TALKS. "Had our monthly statements of account from manufactur-ers included regular ones from Ellis, TALKS would have fared as well as our other books." Meantime accounts for the two psychology books were given "a pretty severe test" for the past twelve years; those for the BRIEFFER COURSE were "accurate to the dot; and the ADVANCED shows a margin of error of only a fraction of one per cent."

In his reply of December 3 James wrote:

My last letter to you at Burlington was based on a misconception by which you have rightly explained to yourself its excessively "strenu-ous" tone. My own unaided genius enabled me to escape from the misconception a couple of hours after I had mailed my letter, but I thought I would await your reply before I sent a postscript.

The misconception was that the figure of "copies subject to royalty," was got, or should be got, from an independent record of sales. This

made me suppose that the sales must needs have been falsified to correspond to the false receipts and that the whole thing must needs have
been deliberate. Your letter and the firm's, ignoring what seemed to
me this obvious circumstance, and harping on "no checks" (when
checks were [and *are*] obviously in your hands) appeared to be concerned attempts to draw my attention away from the direction in
which investigation ought to be pushed, and left me in a state of ab-
solute moral perplexity as to what the game might be.

At last the relieving hypothesis flashed upon me, and was quickly
confirmed by your letters. Sales are accounted for by "receipts" and
"copies on hand" exclusively, with no reference to actual sales-records
at all. This reduced the mystery to carelessness pure and simple, combined with what, from my point of view, I must call an abominably
loose method of ignoring checks on your book-keeping. Ellis's letters
of invoice and your orders to him certainly ought to figure on your
"sheet-book" in place of his bills.

Well! the atmosphere is cleared, and I am glad of it! . . .

Believe me, yours, as ever, W. J.

The nonchalant tone of the letter, in view of the strong accusations of
the previous one, "nonplused" Holt. Referring again to the bookkeeping,
he proceeded to discuss their unfortunate fracas with the acid of repressed anger:

If, before sending you a semi-annual settlement, we had sent you or
Ellis for a semi-annual statement, the errors would have been found,
and the settlement would have been correct, you would not have
imagined sales doctored to conceal stealages, and would have enter-

tained no suspicions that I was trying to take advantage of your in-experience in business to cover up something that would not bear the light, and would not have exhorted me to "stand up and tell the whole truth." Your thinking any of these things when you had our receipts in your hands, is a failure of your intelligence that perplexes me, but what perplexes me more is that, having acknowledged such suspicions to a man with whom you have exchanged salt, and whose reputation, so far as I know, has stood without blemish during a business career of nearly forty years you should, in yours of the 3rd, content yourself, after finding yourself mistaken, with merely calling your remarks "strenuous," expressing satisfaction that "the atmosphere is cleared," and signing the assurance that you are his "as ever."

James's response was a rueful reflection on the factors arousing his suspicions.

The whole thing is perfectly simple to me now, but so long as I conceived of the return of sales being based only on positive entries of all sales made, it threw me into a greater perplexity than I ever remember being thrown into before. If I had only waited a couple of hours before writing that letter on which you animadvert so gracefully in your last, or if you and the firm had only been at the outset as explicit as you afterward became about your usual method of bookkeeping, that letter would certainly never have been written, nor should I now have to apologize for it, as I hereby do. I always explode too abruptly, and I certainly did so in this case. Your tone with me on the contrary has been exemplary, and I only pray you to forgive and forget, yours repentantly.

Holt's acceptance of the apology was gracious: "It's all right and you make it right so manfully that one can hardly regret the occasion. 'Yours as ever' and, I suspect, a little more so."

On December 19, James wrote on a postcard a Christmas greeting: "Let us all thank Heaven that the nightmare episode is over. I am only sorry that it doesn't appear that I have to disgorge anything." Holt replied on the twenty-seventh, "Wishing you a Happy New Year, where publishers shall not vex nor moths break in and steal." James's response on the thirty-first: "Rest, perturbed spirit! and pardon a mind 'perplexed in the extreme' for stirring up so much trouble for you. I feel ashamed of the inordinate extension of my business 'enterprise.' "

A postscript to this agitated episode, nine years later, was Holt's letter of December, 1911, to Professor Leigh R. Gregor, James's brother-in-law. Mr. Burnett, Holt's representative, had reported to the office that Professor Gregor told him that Mrs. James had accused Holt of having treated James unfairly. To set the record straight, Holt sent Gregor copies of the entire correspondence between him and James. He asserted that Mrs. James, "who it is said never to change her mind, made up her mind that I had treated Professor James unfairly, from a set of circumstances which I am now also under the necessity of explaining to you, and has never changed it." He then referred to the Scribner intervention and its consequence. "The matter was finally explained, and although while it was hung up, James took a book to a third publisher, he sent his next one to me. His taking subsequent ones to the third publisher, I have conclusive reason to believe, was not entirely of his own motion." As for Mrs. James's belief that James's Holt contracts "were not as liberal as they ought to have been," the fact was that for the PSYCHOLOGY "our contract with him was substantially the same as with all the eminent men who contributed to the same Series." Nevertheless,

66 James's royalty on the book had later been voluntarily increased. In conclusion Holt asked, "If the misconceptions of all this miserable business under which you have labored, has been conveyed by you to anybody else, is it too much to ask that you now convey the explanation?"

Still later, when William James's son Henry was preparing James's COLLECTED LETTERS, Holt sent him the originals of those in the firm's files and told him that the dispute with his father was "the unhappiest episode in my business career (not to consider my personal relations)." Henry expressed his thanks and added:

> May I therefore seize this occasion to tell you how pleasant my own relations with your firm have been since my father's death, and to say that in going over the accounts and sales figures as I have had to do during the last few years I have been very sensible of the interest and skill that have been devoted to the circulation of my father's books. Long before his death he had dismissed the matter that you refer to as the unfortunate result of unintentional error and misunderstanding.

For reasons best known to himself Henry James did not include any of the letters referring to this episode in the COLLECTED LETTERS. Nor did Professor Ralph Barton Perry make mention of it in his very fine two-volume biography of William James.

VI. Holt's Failures with Popular Authors

For years Holt continued to work "like a tiger"—concentrating on his business during the day and leading an active social life evenings. In the late 1870's his wife suffered a prolonged illness that ended in her death in May, 1879, leaving three young children. By that time Holt was so run down physically and emotionally—he had lost 20 pounds—that his doctor insisted he make a leisurely visit to Europe, in those days a common nostrum for recuperation. Since Vogelius was well able to carry on the routine business of the firm with the aid of Holt's younger brother, Charles, who had recently joined the concern, Holt sojourned in Europe for several months. In the company of his friend John Fiske, he visited Herbert Spencer. He made the personal acquaintance of British authors and publishers, spent a weekend with Turgenev in his villa near Paris and was amazed at the Russian's perfect English, and socialized with the Henry Adamses in Paris. On his return to New York he was again in good health and ready to work with his customary energy.

Shortly after he came back he was made chairman of the University Club library committee. As one of the Club's founders, he took a strong personal interest in its welfare. Heading the committee for seven years, he helped build up the library and made it one of the largest and best private collections in the city. He also devised the bookplate for it. The membership later honored his "great service" to the Club by hanging his portrait prominently in the library.

He resumed his interest in music, which he had studied as a boy but had neglected for many years. He joined the quartet founded by Richard Grant White, the Shakespearean scholar and father of the eminent architect Stanford White. It also included the banker, Joseph W. Drexel. Holt succeeded them as the quartet's cellist and until near the end of his long life he had the group play at his house on Friday evenings—mostly the early Beethoven quartets.

68   In 1886, Holt married Florence Taber. Fond of company for dinner, for which he insisted on dressing as a symbolic means of shedding business cares, he once more resumed his earlier hospitality. The guests he favored, especially those from out of town, he kept overnight and often conversed with until long after midnight. He also thought of acquiring a summer home in upper New England. While stopping in Burlington, Vermont, one day, he was so enchanted with the view of Lake Champlain and the surrounding mountains that he bought a 200-acre tract overlooking the lake. He considered the view more beautiful than that of the Bay of Naples. By 1890, he had a palatial home, named Fairholt, and beautifully landscaped grounds ready for occupancy. William Dean Howells, visiting him some years later, pronounced the place one of the most attractive spots in the world.

Holt arranged to live in Fairholt from April until November—except for moving to Long Island in July and August to be within reach of the office during vacation periods for his staff. His absence did not keep him from maintaining full control of the firm. He made all important decisions by means of daily correspondence. By this time, however, he depended a great deal on Vogelius' good judgment so far as office management went. As his brother Charles, now fully experienced, was of a practical and pessimistic turn of mind, Holt had confidence in his dissents, although he occasionally had to veto some of them. The textbook division was in charge of Edward N. Bristol, who had joined the firm in 1882 and had become thoroughly familiar with the needs of teachers and friendly with those who were likely to write textbooks. Arthur W. Burnett, the first college traveler so designated by a publisher, was proving his able and active associate. In 1890, Holt's son Roland, on graduating from Yale, was taken into the office to thwart his ambition to become an actor—an activity then deeply frowned

upon by respectable families. With these men in the company it became 69
possible for Holt to sojourn at Fairholt, manage his business by correspondence, and devote his free time to his own writing.

With the enactment of the International Copyright Act in 1891, Holt
resumed his interest in English publications. Among the general books
he published through 1901 were Edmund Gosse's poems, ON VIOL
AND FLUTE; Fanny Kemble's three volumes of memoirs; Mill's five
volumes of DISSERTATIONS AND DISCUSSIONS; Victor Duruy's
two-volume history of Europe; E. V. Lucas' THE OPEN ROAD; and
Edward Dowden's PURITAN AND ANGLICAN. In fiction he issued
Jerome K. Jerome's THREE MEN IN A BOAT and a half dozen
other volumes; Anthony Hope's THE PRISONER OF ZENDA, RU-
PERT OF HENTZAU, and five other novels; Henry W. Nevinson's
SLUM STORIES OF LONDON, H. G. Wells's THE TIME MACHINE,
John Buchan's SIR QUIXOTE OF THE MOORS, E. L. Voynich's
THE GADFLY, and George Gissing's OUR FRIEND, THE CHAR-
LATAN.

Holt's publishing ideals and his editorial insistence on good writing—
added to the almost complete breakdown of the "courtesy" principle—
caused him to lose one popular author after another. In 1890, he wrote
to A. P. Watt, one of the first and most influential of English literary
agents, concerning a book that interested him: "If the matter is to be
made in any sense one of competition among publishers, pray spare yourself the trouble of communicating with us any further as we do not
enter into competition." The caustic tone of the letter Watt never forgot.

That April, having published THREE MEN IN A BOAT, which he
had bought from Arrowsmith, the English publisher, without even knowing the author's name, he heard from Jerome that Lovell had made a

tempting offer for his next book. Holt told him what he had said to other English authors, that "Mr. Lovell is one of our most eminent pirates," and was seeking to obtain foreign authors by making them attractive offers. The fact was, however, that Lovell had issued a pirated edition of Jerome's STAGE LAND for 10 cents. Sometime later Holt informed Jerome that "one of the biggest piratical houses is already reported in financial difficulties. The principal man in it has failed twice (we believe) before. Be careful how you are misled by brilliant offers." In January, 1891, Holt wrote that although he was now remitting half of the profits on THREE MEN IN A BOAT, he might have to pay a royalty of only 10 per cent when the sale slackened:

> But on looking over the account, we found that the book had sold more abundantly than we expected. So abundantly as to justify our making this second remittance of one half of the net profits viz. $262— instead of the ten per cent, which would have been only $172.78. You will readily understand that when the sale of the book gets slow, our bother with it is nearly as great as when it is rapid, and that we cannot be justified in paying as liberally under the first set of conditions as under the second. We are glad the second prevailed in this case and hope they will keep up under the influence of your new books.

In March, Holt reported on the new copyright law and asked Jerome to hold up English publication of his new volume until it could also be copyrighted in the United States. "We hope you will now feel encouraged, having both markets, to work with great deliberation, and make your next work a *magnum opus.*"

Holt illustrated the new novel, as was then the custom, but Jerome

and Watt, now his literary agent, were annoyed not to have been con- 71
sulted about the artist. The book did not do well, and Holt balked
when Watt requested an advance of £100 and a royalty of 15 per cent
on the next book; only to yield when Watt threatened to place it with
another publisher. Several years later Watt again requested the same
terms on Jerome's forthcoming novel. This time Holt refused on the
ground that the previous book had not earned that much. "I for one,"
he wrote to Arthur Waugh, who had become his London agent, "have
got through yielding to ridiculous terms for the sake of pleasing Watt
and British authors." What he resented particularly was to have to bid
on a book he had not seen. Thereupon Watt sold the book to Dodd,
Mead and Company, who were ready to pay the advance as well as
up to 20 per cent of list in royalties. Holt was naturally perturbed by
this turn of events. His irritation was aggravated by the thought that
Watt, the agent he disliked most—"there was no place for literary agents
in my impractically ideal relations between established authors and their
established publishers"—had managed to take Jerome away from him.
To Waugh he wrote:

> Can't you make Jerome see through Watt's jumping at the chance
> to sell that book of his away from me? Of course he wanted to break
> up my monopoly of Jerome, as he wants to break up any publisher's
> monopoly of anybody. If you can get me a fair chance at Jerome's
> novel, if it's worth having, I probably can make some sort of arrange-
> ment with Dodd for keeping up some sort of uniform edition; and
> Dodd can't make any arrangement with me: for he has done a ques-
> tionable thing.

A month later Holt told Waugh that he didn't want Jerome "coming
to me reluctantly, and do not let him come back to me as long as any

72 of that spirit lasts." In another letter he stated: "I think with you that Dodd & Mead are running 'enterprise' into the ground. They say, with some apparent pride, that they can sell an edition of 'anything'; but I am confident that if they do it, they do it in virtue of machinery which costs a great deal more than it comes to." When Jerome subsequently suggested to Holt that he drop one of his books, Holt informed Waugh: "To you I say freely (hoping you will say it emphatically to him) that it is rather cheeky of him to ask us to suppress a book of which we have a quantity on hand, for the sake of his other books, when most recent and therefore the most valuable (commercially) of his other books are in the hands of other publishers." When Jerome in 1901 sought to placate Holt by offering him his new book, the response was tardy and unfeignedly cold:

We ought to have answered your letter of Dec. 17 before. Our permitting it to be crowded out by other things has arisen primarily from the delicacy of the situation, but secondarily, we may as well confess, from incapacity to grasp the situation which concerns, so far as we can see, all of an author's future. The present method of distributing that interesting problem among several publishers, divides geometrically the interest that any of them is able to feel in it.

Holt's relation with Anthony Hope likewise ended in frustration. In 1894, he published THE PRISONER OF ZENDA. It became a best seller, went through twenty-six printings in the first year, and sales continued high for many years. Holt and Hope were soon on cordial terms, and five of the author's earlier novels appeared on Holt's list in 1895. Influenced by Watt, however, Hope yielded to the temptations of rival publishers. Informed that Appleton's London agent intended to make

Hope his author and that Stokes had boasted that "the future of Hope's
work is in his hands," Holt strongly resented both Watt's interference
between himself and his author and the latter's greed. Writing in April,
1895, to his earlier representative, Moncure D. Conway, he complained:

> The influence of Watt and some other influences have tended of
> late to prevent authors sticking to one publisher, and have led to a
> general scramble. It is a state of affairs I am sorry for. . . . Anthony
> Hope, although I published the first book that made his reputation
> here, and although he has had the decency to say that he proposes
> to offer me the sequel to it, seems to throw himself open to the
> general scramble.

In March, 1897, Holt agreed to pay Hope £150 on the publication
of RUPERT OF HENTZAU, 15 per cent of list on the first 5,000
copies sold, 17½ per cent on the next 2,500, and 20 per cent thereafter.
In November he wrote to Waugh:

> Stokes announces that he has secured another new book by Anthony
> Hope. This he presumably did from Watt. Do you know the reason
> we did not, considering that we introduced Hope here, publish more
> of his books than anybody else, are promised by him RUPERT OF
> HENTZAU, the sequel to THE PRISONER OF ZENDA, and so
> far as we can make out, are on very pleasant relations with him
> personally.

When Anthony Hope visited the United States, Holt welcomed him
warmly and was his genial host more than once. In January, 1898, he

74　told Hope he was planning a new illustrated edition of THE PRISONER
OF ZENDA uniform with the forthcoming RUPERT OF HENTZAU.
He also suggested the same for DOLLY DIALOGUES, if Hope would
"prepare two or three new Dialogues which we can copyright and pro-
nounce the pirated editions incomplete. How does that strike you?" He
also urged Hope to visit him again before returning to England. "Feel
free to give me short notice any time, should the spirit move you, that
you are ready to lunch with me at the Club or dine with me at home,
if I am free."

Despite Holt's friendly overtures, Hope's new books went to other
publishers. Holt asked Waugh, "I wish you could get at why Watt gives
all Hope-Hawkins things to Appleton or Stokes, except the sequel to
ZENDA, which Hawkins made him give me. I have reason to think their
agents have established a 'pull' on him." Waugh's reply was that Holt
had antagonized Watt by refusing to negotiate with him as Hope's agent.
"No doubt, if you did so with any show of spirit and language—that
would be enough to make Watt chary of you in future."

When Holt received the manuscript of RUPERT OF HENTZAU, he
read it attentively and reacted with keen editorial advice:

Be patient with a suggestion that may strike you as inartistic. I have
an idea that RUPERT would probably sell two or three times as many
if, somehow, "they lived happily ever after," or that it would sell
between its present chances and those brilliant ones if "in death they
were not parted." You can keep the monument and all that, if you
let it cover both of them. You *might* let up on the agony at the last
enough to spare that poor woman's widowhood! I shan't be surprised
if that notion of having the same monument cover both of them
right royally, double action epitaph and all, will satisfy your artistic

sense as well, or even better (oh my cheek!) than the unsociable death
of poor Rassendyll alone.

Hope agreed to change the ending to make his protagonists "live
happily ever after," but rejected the idea of "in death they never parted."
Holt repeated his belief in the validity of the latter scheme which "could
be arranged in a couple of paragraphs; and I am too stupid to see that
it would be inartistic. But you are not as stupid as I am." Acquiescing
in Hope's refusal, Holt published RUPERT in July, 1898, with an advance sale of 20,000 copies. Although the novel did not do nearly as
well as ZENDA, it outsold Hope's other novels. In addition to the
cloth-bound editions Holt arranged with the American News Company
and later with other reprinters for cheap editions of ZENDA, amounting to 214,250 copies. He had Grosset and Dunlap bring out RUPERT
in a cheaper edition, totaling 60,000 copies.

In his correspondence with Hope and especially with Watt, Holt was
frequently exasperated by their unco-operativeness and their disregard
of anything but money. Yet he graciously tried to arrange for a uniform
edition of Hope's works despite the fact that his novels had become
scattered among American publishers. His effort failed—proving his
insistence that an author cannot auction off his books to the highest
bidders and enjoy the pleasure of a uniform edition.

Mrs. E. L. Voynich was an even greater disappointment. The daughter
of William Boole, the eminent mathematician, she married a Lithuanian
exile whose ill health made residence in the warm climate of Italy highly
desirable. In need of money, Mrs. Voynich turned to writing and in
due course completed THE GADFLY, a novel about revolution in Italy.
Published in England by Heinemann without much success, THE GAD-

76 FLY, Holt told Waugh subsequently, "was offered to every other respectable publisher in New York, and possibly some not respectable, before it was offered to me." He read it without prejudice, agreed to pay £30 advance and 10 per cent royalty, and published it in 1896. Its reception was critically auspicious and its sale increased with the passing months, over 3,000 copies in December, 1898. With this book in mind, Holt wrote to Waugh at that time, "The impression grows stronger in me that more people want a good thing in America than in England, and that there are not so many here as with you, who will take a poor thing or a merely average thing at any price."

The success of THE GADFLY caused a number of American publishers—nine in all—to go after Mrs. Voynich's next book, much to Holt's chagrin. Waugh reported that since she had to support a sick husband, Mrs. Voynich was inclined to accept the best offer. "Pawling [her English editor] thinks it would immensely strengthen your hold upon her if you would express your willingness to cancel the agreement [on THE GADFLY] and pay her 12½ from January 1." Holt agreed to the increase of 2½ per cent royalty and offered 15 per cent on the first 5,000 copies of the new novel, 17½ on the next 2,500, and 20 thereafter, as well as an advance of £150. He added, "If my figures above do not get the book, telegraph me before letting it go elsewhere; tho I probably should not go higher in any event." He also expressed his readiness to give 20 per cent royalty on the new illustrated edition of THE GADFLY.

Complications in connection with the dramatization of THE GADFLY brought Mrs. Voynich to New York. Holt had her as his house guest and did everything possible to protect her stage rights in the play. He also arranged with the CENTURY MAGAZINE for the serialization of her new novel. "Our intention of offering it to you," he wrote to the editor subsequently, "has never varied. You know how uncertain the movements of authors are. The MS. may be here any day, and it may not be here for a good while to come."

When the manuscript of the new novel reached him, he found it artistically deficient in certain respects and advised revision in the light of his critical suggestions. Mrs. Voynich disagreed with him about the merits of the story and refused to make any changes in it. Waugh informed him:

> Mrs. Voynich . . . said with great regret, that the situation, so far as you were concerned, was hopeless. She declines to alter a word, and feels therefore, that the work must go elsewhere for America. She said she was very sorry for this since she had the greatest regard for you personally and had hoped to have all her books with you. She still intends to offer you her next book, when, in the course of years, it is ready. The present book is now offered to Doubleday and Page.

The next thing Holt learned, from Doubleday, was that Mrs. Voynich had agreed to make changes for him. In righteous anger he wrote to her, "Of course your refusing to revise for me, and then sending the book revised to another publisher, is something that my imagination cannot explain. I will have to await explanation from you." Waugh, on learning that Mrs. Voynich had only made a few minor stylistic emendations and was deeply hurt by Holt's letter, wrote in her defense:

> As I anticipated, Doubleday has quite misrepresented the case to you. I am not surprised that this should be so, because my own impression of Doubleday, which may of course be perfectly unjust, is that he is one of the finest braggarts and boasters that ever came out

of America. . . . It is not true that Mrs. Voynich is making any corrections in her book which can be described as a result of any criticism either of Pawling, yourself, or anyone else.

True to her promise, Mrs. Voynich late in 1903 sent the manuscript of her new novel to Henry Holt. As before, he readily accepted it and offered her 10 per cent on the first 2,500 copies sold, 15 per cent on the next 2,500, and 20 per cent thereafter. She asked for a large advance and better terms, but he refused, telling her to go to another publisher if one offered her more. And having read the manuscript with his usual critical care, he suggested certain emendations. Again Mrs. Voynich balked, and wrote him in February, 1904: "What made me feel that our points of view were utterly incompatible was your asking me to 'let you cut out,' as 'pretty but unnecessary' the final scene, which I regard as the keystone to the whole book, and which has cost me more to write than I can tell you."

Holt's forthright reply well stated his position as editor:

My suggestion to you to cut out or put in or change, was simply a suggestion for your consideration, and in no sense a requirement; and I cannot realize my having made the suggestions as legitimately bearing at all on the question of your withdrawing the MS.

I have reason to believe that I offer more suggestions regarding MSS. than publishers generally do, and perhaps I have also reason to believe that a larger percentage of my suggestions is taken, than that of publishers in general; whether to the benefit of authors or not, of course there is no means of determining.

Again the novel went to another publisher.

Her later novels achieved not even a modicum of the popularity of THE GADFLY, but the relations between Holt and Mrs. Voynich were broken. Meanwhile the sale of her first novel continued high, and it remained on the Holt list for many years. In addition one cheap printing of 50,000 copies was made in 1900 and another for the same number was issued in 1912. In recent years the Russian and Chinese Communists have made much of the novel because of its favorable account of a revolution.

Holt's experience with Paul Leicester Ford, an American author, was no more rewarding. Badly crippled, Ford received no formal education; but making his father's extensive library his university, he became highly erudite. He edited the writings of a number of eminent Americans and also wrote fiction. In 1894, he submitted the manuscript of THE HONORABLE PETER STIRLING to Holt, who liked the novel, but was skeptical enough of its salability to require of Ford a deposit of money as a guarantee that the book would sell a thousand copies within three years. The work, a sociological novel that to some extent foreshadowed the muckraking fiction of the 1900's, sold better than Holt had anticipated, totaling 1,500 copies during the first eighteen months.

In June, 1895, in reply to Ford's inquiry concerning the nature of publishing, Holt wrote to him at length. He explained what happened to a manuscript after it reached a publisher, the function of publisher's readers, usually intelligent librarians eager to earn 50 to 75 cents an hour by reading and reporting on manuscripts during their free time. No manuscript, however, was accepted on the opinion of only one reader.

In fact in this shop no book is taken on any one verdict but my own, and mighty seldom at that; I generally preferring in the very rare instances where for some personal reason I attack a MS. at first hand, to see how it will strike somebody else, though I did send CALLED BACK, THREE MEN IN A BOAT, and THE PRISONER OF ZENDA to press of my own independent notion.

When a book has been published six months, and you see an advertisement of it from this shop, as you may today in the TIMES, TRIBUNE, and POST, you can know that the book has some life in it. STIRLING is now selling an average of about 30 a week.

When you get your other book done, don't you be going off to other publishers with it after you have found fame under my wing—unless of course you are making on an order from Harper.

At about this time A. M. Robinson, a San Francisco bookseller, came to believe that Peter Stirling was a disguised portrait of President Grover Cleveland and ordered 100 copies. His enthusiasm infected his regular customers and soon other people began to buy the book. Before long the news traveled to Denver, to Chicago, to Cleveland, and finally to New York. Everywhere the book sold in quantity. For the next four years the novel was a best seller at the regular price of $1.50. In 1899, a cheap edition limited to 100,000 copies found a ready market. Six years later another printing of 75,000 was put on sale. Grosset and Dunlap issued its own edition of 15,250 in 1909 and another of 20,500 in 1914. All the while Holt kept the regular edition in print and by 1945, fifty years after publication, it was in its seventy-sixth printing—totaling a half million copies.

In 1896, Holt learned that Ford had given his new novel to Dodd, Mead. After telling him how well STIRLING was doing, Holt continued in quiet anger:

Perhaps even your modesty will not prevent your realizing that I find the fact of your having placed the MS. of your new book (which you had already spoken of to me) in the hands of another firm, a disagreeable surprise. I hope that your doing so has not arisen from any dissatisfaction with our handling of your old one. If it has not, the result of your publishing elsewhere (if you do so), would do us injustice, as the literary public will inevitably assume the dissatisfaction, whether it exists or not.

The fact that Dodd, Mead and Co. would endeavor to get serial rights for you hardly seems to cover the situation. We could make that endeavor just as easily as they; and talk of anybody having a pull on a magazine that it's worth while to have a pull on, is nonsense: for if anybody had, the magazine would not be worth the pull.

Ford's explanation did not appease Holt and his acknowledgment, while cordial, was caustic. Some weeks later he informed Ford that so eminent a critic as Professor George Baker of Harvard had written to the firm: "I have never told you, I think, how deeply I have enjoyed PETER STIRLING. I have recommended it widely, and in nearly all cases to the satisfaction of the readers. I look forward much to meeting Mr. Ford at Christmas." In February, 1897, while writing to him on another matter, Holt added, "If you have been wasting your patrimony and need something on account of royalty, tell us how much, but don't tell us too much." He also prodded Ford regarding a decision on a proposed edition of THE FEDERALIST, which Ford finally agreed to do without delay.

The final letter to Ford, written by a member of the Holt firm, is a peculiar climax to the oscillating author-publisher relationship. Ford had

82 exploded in anger when presented with a bill for excessive alterations. The reply of November 1, 1898, follows:

> Your letter of October 26 being such as we are not accustomed to receiving from gentlemen, or from anybody, we have delayed answering it until we could refer it to the head of the firm who is absent.
>
> Though you say that you have published seventy books without receiving a bill for alterations, PETER STIRLING was, we believe, your first novel, and THE FEDERALIST you did not see through the press yourself. Be all that as it may, however, we have published more than seven times seventy books, have rendered a bill for alterations every time they were excessive (which has not been seldom), and have never before received a letter deciding the case against us without investigation. Nor have we ever before, under any circumstances that we can remember, even from some writer vastly less able to express himself than you are, [received] a letter containing a passage which could justifiably, whether correctly or not, be interpreted as an attempt at blackmail.
>
> Such a letter, while permitted to stand, of course renders discussion or even explanation impossible.

Though not signed by Henry Holt, the letter bears the imprint of his caustic style and gentlemanly indignation. It deliberately severed a relationship that had begun very amicably. Ford's reply retracted the curt tone about the charges and stated that some of them should have been borne by the firm, but there is no indication of any acknowledgment.

VII. Holt's English Agents

Every sizable American publisher sooner or later engaged an English representative to serve him in Great Britain. It was this agent's function to acquaint the publisher with forthcoming books, to approach authors who might interest American readers, to be on friendly terms with British publishers and literary agents, and in general to be his employer's eyes and ears in England. The efficiency of these representatives, most of whom were authors or publishers, varied considerably; some never earned their salaries or commissions, while several greatly augmented the business of their employers.

Henry Holt engaged men of literary prominence to act for him in England, men who served him only middlingly and who, despite their intimacy with him, wholly ignored him in their published memoirs. His first agent, Moncure Conway, an American clergyman and man of letters, lived in London and had previously represented Harper & Brothers. Holt, having published his book on demonology, asked him in 1871 to serve him in England. Although he soon discovered that Conway had little business shrewdness, Holt retained him for many years.

The first book Conway sent Holt was already taken by Appleton. Not to discourage him, Holt explained how these things happened. After several months Holt sent him a draft for £50 as compensation and hoped it would soon be more. He also asked him to find out if THE FORTNIGHTLY REVIEW had previously been handled by an American house. "I have no doubt that its sale could be quadrupled by a little pushing. . . . I would take strong personal interest in giving our people widely the benefit of that admirable periodical." Conway provided him with the desired information. Holt then arranged with Chapman and Hall, publishers of the REVIEW, to assume the American agency for it. He promoted it at a loss for more than two years, but finally gave it up as a hopeless cause.

84   Conway continued to send books and news from England, but little came of them. In 1877, Holt told him he was ready to pay £200, two months after publication, as an advance on Froude's biography of Carlyle, and if the book sold over 5,000 copies, a royalty of 10 per cent. He cautioned him, however, that "trade courtesy" made it necessary to discuss the project with Scribner, who had already published Froude; and when Scribner refused to give up the book, Holt yielded. To prod Conway's son Eustace, who had temporarily taken over his father's work, to greater activity, Holt told him that watching the reviews was not enough. "Most of the good books," he pointed out, "are brought down for some American publisher while they are still in the air, long before they have come down into the definite form of a printed volume. The ideal plan is when anything good is rumored, to 'go after it.' That's American too." Eustace, however was no more a businessman than his father and was relieved to give up the scouting.

As late as 1895, Holt advised Conway, whose services he still used occasionally, that since Sheldon of Appleton was trying to take Anthony Hope, his action "can legitimately cancel any squeamishness you may have about what may otherwise appear his preserves, and should you ever intrench upon it to a degree that Appleton and we agree in thinking excessive, the difficulty can be settled here." By that time, however, Conway was too old to exert himself to any extent.

In March, 1878, Holt approached George Bentley, a friendly English publisher, for help as his representative. "Why wouldn't it be legitimate for you to act for me in London as I understand Sampson Low & Co. do for Harpers—*i.e.*, keep them posted regarding books that are likely to suit them and arrange for such as require negotiation on the spot?" Holt explained that Conway's other interests were absorbing him, "and moreover he was never made for business." Even so, he pointed out, Conway received over £100 a year "as his share of the plunder for the first two years." Bentley, having a wide acquaintance as well as business ability, might with very little trouble earn much more. "I think that you have a fair idea of what sort of books would suit me. I am very particular, you know, on the question of literary execution. I sometimes suspect too much so for my own advantage. But the range of topics and opinions I welcome is large."

Bentley agreed to help Holt. The first request was for Bentley to suggest to Mrs. Alexander, Holt's popular novelist, "to let an American friend make a few touches in the MS. of everything she may do hereafter, so that we can copyright it here and choke off the pirates. This will make a difference of many a solid pound in her receipts as well as ours from the next books."

Early in 1879, Holt wrote Bentley a long, chatty letter about their several transactions as well as about general publishing conditions. He complained especially about the piratical reprinters who had issued a cheap edition of Wallace's RUSSIA, which he had published at great expense and promoted vigorously. "Now so many people are getting used to a good day's reading for ten cents, that very few will pay more for it."

Holt's visit to England later that year served to strengthen his relations with Bentley, though the result in books was insignificant, owing mainly to Holt's exceptionally high standards. In September, 1880, replying to Bentley's query about the Harpers, Holt wrote:

The present generation of Harpers is a great improvement on the first one. It's not to my interest to praise my competitors, so you will know what weight to attach to my saying that for some of them—especially for J. W. Jr., the present head of the house—I have a very high regard indeed. Take all of their money that you can get; there's not much money so clean.

In December, 1882, Holt informed Bentley that he was planning to start the Leisure Moment Series "to compete with the pirates," and asked him to be on the lookout for good short novels. "Anything, new or old, by any good author that you may be able to send, will be highly appreciated. . . . Of course, if we make any money from anything of that kind, we shan't forget you." When Holt thought in 1884 that the copyright law was about to be passed, he asked Bentley to send him "title pages of anything new," and he would, as soon as the law went into effect, deposit them in Washington. "Then as soon as the books are ready, if the telegraph reports to you that the law is passed, send me four copies of each book, two for the Library of Congress and two to be used either for me to work from, in your interest, or to dispose of your rights in case I cannot use the books myself." This friendly relationship became quiescent with the passing of the years; later correspondence between these two concerned only their separate publishing interests.

In 1897, Holt engaged Arthur Waugh, English critic and publisher, as his London representative at a salary of £200 a year plus expenses. Their frequent correspondence dealt as much with publishing gossip as with business matters. Holt, not wishing to discourage Waugh at the outset, told him that since Watt "holds the field so far as the disposal of the works of the best known novelists," and since he arranged for several books in advance, "it will not be easy, with the best of luck, to get work from writers of the calibre of Doyle, Anthony Hope, Ian Maclaren, Crocket or the like for a couple of years from the present date." Somewhat later, in reply to another letter, Waugh wrote:

I will be as candid as you ask. No one seems to have the slightest apprehension in placing any book with you, but their negative argument is that you are so cautious that whatever they submit is likely to be declined. They say—"But don't you think we shall only be losing time? We must place the book soon, and Mr. Holt always declines everything." The only other argument I have heard against doing business is a query whether your house is enterprising enough, whether it is not, in a certain solid and dignified sense, too old-fashioned.

Waugh offered J. K. Huysmans' LA CATHEDRALE to Holt and praised it highly, but the latter did not find it to his taste—considering himself much more discriminating than Heinemann, its English publisher. Waugh complained:

Heinemann's taste, you say, is not very high; but still it is the taste that pays. His business is one of the healthiest in London. I am discouraged to have offered you so little that has been palatable, but every fresh refusal gives me new insight into the kind of thing you do *not* want, so that soon I expect I shall be as "destructive" in my attude as the advisers of your N.Y. office.

When Waugh informed Holt that English publishers considered him too slow in reaching decisions, his annoyed response was that many of them were "raging lunatics." They kept American books for weeks without coming to any decision, yet sent him "shreds of books and single volumes of series" and wanted a decision within a week. "Now I am heartily sick of this, and indignant at it; and I wish you would arm yourself with a big club and pound into them the reasons which justify my being sick and indignant." He assured Waugh that Heinemann's taste was not "a determining factor in my business." He also declared that English publishers were in a hurry over books that Waugh "can very easily satisfy them by rejecting the books on the spot"; that they were not in any hurry over books "of real importance here . . . and I don't want to see any other books." As it was, he continued, they only sent the books "they can't get rid of to American agents in London," and he was not interested in "twaddle." He hoped that Waugh was not discouraged by this attitude, and ended his long letter by stating that most current fiction did not interest him, "but I hope you will be able to learn from publishers which of such books are worth your looking at, and get the chance to look at them well in advance and send me the one in fifty which seems worth the attention of a being with a soul."

Writing again the next day, in reply to a letter just received, Holt was more relaxed and sought to pacify Waugh by admitting that he was "apt to fall into great blunders regarding matters as far off as London . . . and your setting me straight is a real service." He was certain nevertheless that English publishers brought out novels inferior to those "demanded by American publishers of equal standing." In response to Waugh's query he expressed his *a priori* views of the American market for books:

Our really cultured class is not nearly as large as yours, although our practically educated class is, I suppose, vastly larger. As for a leisure class, we have none; and even those whose interest would delight in leisure, are now crowded by excessive activities, into being men "of few books." This is true even of the professors in our colleges. Nearly all have to do so much teaching that it is hard for them to keep up with their subjects, let alone make original investigations.

A day later he wrote again. "It is important that you should get in-
side of my mind regarding choice books for publication, as far as possible." He pointed out that in the six months of their relationship the
result was not very fruitful for obvious reasons, that he was sent "a
good many books which were really not worth considering," and if it
weren't "a dangerous doctrine," he would prefer to receive only six
books "out of which I could get three good ones." He also urged him
to cultivate Watt—on this matter he blew hot and cold at intervals—and
even more the newer writers of fiction, history, and belles-lettres. "Of
course an important function of any person acting in England for an
American publisher is to keep the English publishers reminded of the
American publisher's existence; but another important function is learning through literary associations of promising things, before the publishers have anything to say about them." In another letter he boasted that
"twenty years ago I was next to Harpers as a novel publisher in the
United States, and it was all done in new men."

Waugh, finding it difficult to satisfy Holt, accused him of shifting po-
sitions. "Don't think I'm angry. I'm not. But your letters show so little
satisfaction with me that I really feel you ought to know that I am rather
more intelligent than you think." Holt quickly disabused him of this
complaint. He assured him that although his concrete accomplishments
were not enough, "estimated in money, to pay for postage, I nevertheless
told my partner the other day that having you to call on for intelligent
information and intermediaryship, is a great comfort."

In June, 1898, Holt wrote, "I don't think I've made you understand
yet that I don't publish anything that I don't think is good, no matter
how well it is expected to sell. My dear old friend George Bentley urged
and urged me to publish Marie Corelli, telling me that I would make
lots of money out of it. It was probable that I would, but I absolutely

and reiteratedly refused." A month later Waugh informed him that Appleton "seemed to have been drawing in their horns a good deal," refusing Sir John Lubbock's new book in spite of the success of his earlier work in the International Scientific Series. Holt, however, was not interested in it. When Waugh told him that W. W. Jacobs' new novel required an advance of £200, Holt replied that £100 was enough and that he would have to see the manuscript first. Dodd, however, did not ask to see the manuscript before giving the requested advance. A little later, when Waugh expressed surprise that Holt had let Putnam have Leslie Stephen's new book, Holt explained:

> If you had been here in one of the leading publishing houses, you wouldn't be so much surprised at my transfer of the Stephen book to Putnam. Before the International Copyright Law, the best publishing houses here found that the extreme of courtesy in regard to books on which any one of them had a claim, was on the whole better policy than the game of grab; and among a few the tradition survives, where it is backed up by pleasant personal relations, although not with the vigor that it had in the old times when it had some of sanctions of honor among thieves.

In his next letter Holt pointed out that there was a time when "it was possible for a publisher, even in his capacity of publisher, to succeed and still be a gentleman. This maneuvering of publishers to get each other's authors away has of course killed all that, but I manage to make a pretty comfortable living without doing any of it." Several months later, interested in a novel whose author had been published by Appleton, Holt nevertheless cautioned Waugh against going after it; but, he added, should anything of this author "be legitimately put within your reach

without your seeking it, I should be sorry to let it slip." Yet he continued to believe that "it is almost as important for an author to put
probably *all* his books under the critical care of a competent publisher
as it is for him to take similar relations in some trusted doctor, lawyer
and (if he feels the need, for which I should pity him) parson."

For all his efforts, Waugh failed to reconcile Watt toward Holt. Watt
told him, rather unfairly, that Holt "always expects me to get the sure
successes and does not take a very large share of the risks." Waugh
only told Holt, "I *do* think that your readers reject an unusually large
percentage of fairly promising stuff." Moreover, Holt's terms of no
royalties on the first 1,000 copies of a book by a new author and double
royalties on the second 1,000 were "unpalatable" to English authors
and publishers. Holt countered with the statement that other publishers
might take a certain amount of "tommy-rot, but I am Pharisee enough
to thank God that I am not as most people in this respect. Perhaps I
take some tommy-rot too, but never under any circumstances if I know
it." In a later letter he elaborated: "I don't believe we are a hard concern
to do business with. At all events, I have been in business nearly thirty-
five years, and have, on the whole, made more money each year than
the year before, which would seem to indicate that, roughly speaking,
more people have been willing to do business with us than the year
before."

Early in 1899, Waugh wrote that Appleton had given Sarah Grand, a
popular novelist, £1,000 advance and a high royalty for the book rights
to her new novel; that Dominick of Stokes paid £150 advance on
Jacobs' book. "I suppose," Waugh remarked, "this rotten way of doing
business will go on until a few plungers have burned their fingers sufficiently."

In May, Holt told Waugh that his wife, "who is a poetry sharp," has been reading the sheets of E. V. Lucas' THE OPEN ROAD and liked the book, so that he was willing to publish it. At the same time he said sarcastically, "You are right in your impression that I am not at present in business for the sake of buying pigs in pokes which are being raised by men in asylums." He also informed him that H. B. Claflin Company, "our leading dry goods jobbers," bought 30,000 sets of Kipling from Doubleday, McClure and Company. "The H. B. C. Co. have added a book department to their business, supplying of course the book departments now generally characteristic of the 'department stores.' They lately bought a hundred thousand ZENDA and a hundred thousand STIRLING from us in paper, to be retailed at 50 cents."

The following month Holt commented on the ephemeral union of Harper with Doubleday and McClure:

> I myself am meditating more and more upon the "commercialization of literature," which of course includes restricting the publishing business more and more to the pure (or impure) dollars-and-cents relations. The most startling illustration of this that I can recall, is the virtual blending of Harper's house with McClure's, which was announced in yesterday's papers. I think if my dear old friend, Joe Harper, had been alive, it wouldn't have happened. He had some old-fashioned notions of family pride and professional (?) pride, and that sort of thing.

In his next letter Holt said he was puzzled to receive anything by Ouida, a popular novelist. What he knew about her had convinced him that she was not his type of author. "While I am very fond of making money, I am equally fond of making it in my own way, and in feeling comfortable in the possession of any that I may obtain; and I am such

a crank that those results seem to require a good deal of deference to
what I consider good taste as well as good morals!" Not long after he
complained, "I do hate the condition of the publishing business which
has made me tolerate the idea of taking FOLLY CORNER if Macmillan wants it; but we seemed to have reached that condition where
dog must eat dog or starve." And again, tired of dickering with Watt,
he advised Waugh "to tell him as euphemistically as you please, that
there is no use in his bringing any more of his refuse matter to us—
that we don't deal in it. He brings nothing else."

Waugh's next batch of letters stated, among other things, that Appleton was very slow to arrive at a decision, and that "if it were not that
Appleton has a peculiarly good name for selling books I do not think
that Sheldon would enjoy the large field he does"; that Max Pemberton,
the Dodd agent, bought books "in a somewhat slap-dash fashion"; that
Heinemann had often told him "that for a certain class of sound and
solid work he would sooner have you as the American publisher than
anyone."

The following letter by Holt to Waugh concerning the Harper failure
in 1899 provides a salient aspect of publishing conditions at the turn
of the century:

Speaking of paying down, I wonder if the Harpers have had enough
of it, and how long it will take to get a similar demonstration that
some other houses here have had enough. The cause of Harper's
failure was sheer lack of capacity. Three generations had dwindled
it all out. Harry Harper is a good fellow and a man of some ability,
but not ability enough to "swing" his cousins, or to know that his
house was bankrupt when it was. He couldn't believe it when Doubleday found it out and told him so. One of the forms that the incapacity

has taken has been the holding onto Harpers and other people in all sorts of unnecessary and expensive capacities, and no new blood was taken into the actual management, as has been done in the case of Macmillan. The house may go on again under the same name, tho it was rather a queer move for Morgan, the banker, who held the principal claim, to take for a manager, a man Harvey, editor of the NORTH AMERICAN REVIEW, who had had no experience in book publishing, and very little in any other kind of publishing, except some in early life in a newspaper. . . .

I am moved to say that the extravagance in plunging and advertising, among American publishers, has lately been a sheer madness; and had the Harpers not tried to keep up with that sort of thing, and sometimes possibly lead it, they might have lasted perhaps until there had grown up some Harper capable of managing the concern. As you know, we have kept out of it (not the Harpers, but the plunging), and have lost in some respects by doing so; and yet I am not at all sure that any American publisher who dabbles in miscellaneous books, has had, on the whole, more occasion to be satisfied with his business for some years past, than we have. I don't mean miscellaneous business alone: for in America, at least, I don't think any house has been able to live on miscellaneous business alone, for many years. First it was rendered impossible by piracy, and now it has become impossible by insanities of competition.

In March, 1900, Holt also animadverted on the Appleton receivership. "The present generation are hard-working fellows with a passable amount of business capacity, and the state of affairs is attributed to no special fault of theirs." Although the two failures, he added rather smugly, would no doubt cause bankers to take "a very skeptical view regarding

publishers . . . it makes little difference to us. Our firm has not a dollar
under discount, and we are ourselves discounting our time obligations."
Two months later Holt reiterated his frequent complaint about his
English business.

I am gradually becoming near sure that the amount of time that
I have spent in reference to the English market for a good many
years past, has not paid me either as a publisher or as a human being,
and I don't believe that the time so spent has paid anybody else,
even Appleton or Harper, who have had more good English things
probably than all the rest of us put together. . . . In the old days,
when the relation of publisher and author amounted to that of a trusted
professional man and his habitual client, I used to care a little something for the business. I am rapidly becoming disgusted with it—not
that income has not kept up: for income is not the only thing in life,
and tho income has kept up, it has been kept up by other things than
the time and pain devoted to the English market.

Having published George Gissing's OUR FRIEND, THE CHARLA-
TAN, Holt also liked his new novel, THE COMING MAN, but objected to the sexual and sensual parts which have "been used so crassly
not to say excessively in recent literature," and urged "a little dilution."
Referring also to James Pinker's request for an advance on the novel,
he told Waugh: "I am opposed to the general principle of payment in
advance. There is no reason in the world why an author should not
take the risks that the publisher does in the matter of royalty. A sliding
scale of royalty that will make the author's remuneration very large if
the publisher's is, fulfils every requirement of justice." When he was
finally ready to give the advance of £100, Pinker messed matters up

96   by giving the novel to another publisher—much to Holt's annoyance. Some time later, elaborating on his ideas toward advances, Holt modified his position considerably:

> I should much rather that Gissing's hundred pound book had been a thousand pound book, and I am entirely ready to go large sums on any books that warranted it—would vastly prefer to. Perhaps you have not realized this. My only hesitation about going large sums is where they are asked for doubtful books. It is perfect nonsense that Stokes should be handling bigger matters than we do. Without wishing to appear arrogant in any way, I suppose there is no sort of question that we are ten or probably twenty times as strong as he is; and how our strength compares with Harpers or Appletons, you know. In fact, I do not suppose it is immodest for me to say that Scribner is the only New York publisher competing in the English market whose financial standing is at all to be compared with ours.

Once more returning to advances a little later, Holt asked Waugh: "Pray disabuse Arrowsmith of his idea that I shall stick to the resolution I formed in other ages, of not paying anything in advance of royalty. As you know, I am willing to pay anything a book is worth."

Early in 1902, Holt's annoyance with Watt again boiled over. He asked Waugh if the agent had a sense of humor—sending him worthless books despite repeated rejections. "Will you please stop right where you are, spending any of your time on the sort of stuff that Watt sends us, and tell him that I told you to do so. . . . Now that I have worked my mad off, I leave to you to determine whether it is best to do as I say. . . . I think he may just as well understand in plain English that I don't want to be made a fool of any longer." Subsequently he wrote

to Waugh that there was a time when Watt could find some American
publishers fools enough to do anything he proposed, but that no longer
was the case. "My mournful attendance at his funeral is only a question
of time. Small and Maynard have just failed, Stone is doing next to
no business, Stokes says he is entirely sick of novels, Appleton told me
that he and Dodd have both about concluded to agree not to bother
any more with serial rights." Waugh refrained from telling Holt that
he had a high opinion of Watt. Years later he wrote that Watt "set his
successors and rivals a distinguished example of integrity, sound judgment, and fair negotiation between client and customer." That Watt and
Holt remained at odds was the fault as much of one as of the other—
both being proud and principled men unyielding in matters of policy.

Holt was now vacillating between giving up the English market and
sending over an American of his choice. He intimated to Waugh, "I am
utterly sick of the publishing business as now conducted. This haste
and competition over literary matters, as if they were shares of stock
or barrels of pork, is not what I went into the business to participate
in." His dismissal of Waugh was on the friendliest terms, and with
business being slack, he was in no hurry to send his new representative
to London. Indeed for many years he had no agent there; he depended
on his correspondence with English publishers until he was ready to send
Alfred Harcourt on periodic visits to England.

VIII. Holt's Activities in the 1900's

98 Although Henry Holt had, in the 1890's begun delegating the routine work of the office to his several associates, he continued to control the firm's policies and major decisions. In the exercise of his prerogative as head of the house, he remained loyal to his early ideals and principles. Perspicacious, practical, increasingly conservative, concentrating more and more on his own writing, he nevertheless persisted in his vain effort to give publishing the status of a profession. He despised haggling for manuscripts, vulgar advertising, and exaggerated promotion. In rejecting a manuscript in May, 1899, he wrote, "It won't do for a publisher whose aims are what mine are, to offer the 'trade' unsuccessful books. The reputation with the trade of publishing 'sellers' is very important to maintain, and doubly difficult to maintain for a house which will not willingly take trash for the sake of getting 'sellers.' "

Holt continued to adhere to the "courtesy" principle. When he learned that Grant Richards had already submitted Samuel Butler's EREWHON to Lippincott, he would not examine his copy until Lippincott had given it up. In 1902, he cautioned his trade editor, F. S. Hackett, against going after authors of other publishers. "It is utterly opposed to my habits and the old-fashioned sense of dignity of the business, and I am pretty old to learn." Yet he did not feel that restriction with publishers who had tried to take away his authors. In another letter to Hackett he said, "As to [George] Ade: Stone once made a direct effort to get one of my authors, and the more you can get from him, the better. I have something of the same feeling regarding Dodd & Mead."

Nor did he hesitate to propose projects to authors who had already published elsewhere. In 1900, he approached Professor William M. Sloane, who at times had read manuscripts for him, to contribute a volume on the French Revolution to a projected history series. Knowing that Sloane had connections with other publishers, he wrote: "Of course

you will begin by saying No—men worth having almost always do,
but I don't want you to write No. I want you to wait even to say it,
until we can talk the subject over, and I write now so that you can
think the No away meanwhile."

In 1902, he wrote to John Kendrick Bangs regarding the DIARY
OF PRINCE HENRY that if he were not committed to his regular
publisher, "I should be very glad to publish for you, if you would be
glad to have me, and of course would hope to make the results mutually
satisfactory." Similarly, when Bristol informed him that Professor Remsen was writing an ADVANCED ORGANIC CHEMISTRY but felt an
obligation to Heath, the publisher of his smaller book in the subject,
Holt advised that Remsen tell Heath that "since the course of circumstance of many years had made his interests with us considerable, he
would like to have all his books on Holt's list and wondered if Heath
would mind transferring the ORGANIC CHEMISTRY to Holt. Of
course nothing should be said about the new book."

Spurred and assisted by Holt, Bristol developed a textbook list of high
quality and wide acceptance in every major area of college study. The
textbook department was especially strong in psychology. When John B.
Watson, whose BEHAVIORISM Holt had published, wanted the firm
to bring out his elementary text, he wrote, "You have published every
introductory text in the country that has had any success." Equally important was the American Historical Series, edited by Charles H. Haskins
of Harvard. Among the contributors were Charles D. Hazen, Preserved
Smith, W. R. Shepherd, Tenney Frank, George B. Adams—all scholars
of distinction. Concurrently the firm published widely adopted texts in
the American Mathematical Series, edited by E. J. Townsend of Illinois.
In the 1920's, Bristol arranged for three additional series: the American
Business Series, edited by Dean R. C. McCrea of Columbia; the Ameri-

can Political Science Series, edited by Edward S. Corwin of Princeton; and the American Social Science Series, edited by Howard W. Odum of North Carolina.

In the high-school field the firm was particularly successful with English Readings, British and American classics reprinted in well-edited and inexpensive editions. Equally popular were the English texts by Alfred M. Hitchcock, the texts in chemistry and physics by Charles E. Dull, the accounting books by Harry A. Finney, BIOLOGY FOR BE-GINNERS by T. J. Moon, COMMERCE AND INDUSTRY by J. Russell Smith, and several mathematics books.

Holt's leadership in foreign language texts was maintained throughout most of this period, D. C. Heath being the strongest rival. The texts in French, German, Spanish, and Italian were highly regarded by teachers everywhere.

Satisfied with Bristol's management of the textbook division, Holt devoted most of his working time to trade books. He carried on a wide correspondence with authors and with British publishers and agents. His "courtesy" and conservatism notwithstanding, he managed to publish a commendable list: notably August Fournier's NAPOLEON THE FIRST (1903); Gabriel Tarde's THE LAWS OF IMITATION (1903); C. M. and A. M. Williamson's THE LIGHTNING CONDUCTOR (1903); B. E. Stevenson's THE HOLLADAY CASE (1903) and AFFAIRS OF STATE (1906); Stopford Brooks's LECTURES ON SHAKE-SPEARE (1905); May Sinclair's THE DIVINE FIRE (1905) and three later novels; L. T. Hobhouse's MORALS IN EVOLUTION (1907); John Dewey's INFLUENCE OF DARWINISM ON PHILOSOPHY (1909); Henri Bergson's CREATIVE EVOLUTION (1910); J. Arthur Thomson's DARWINISM AND HUMAN LIFE (1910); Romain Rolland's JEAN CHRISTOPHE (1910–1913); and dozens of other volumes of merit.

The Holt list included a good many children's books. J. D. Champlin's YOUNG FOLKS' CYCLOPEDIA OF COMMON THINGS, in four volumes, was a standard and popular work. Among the other widely sold juveniles were the books for boys by C. P. Burton and also by M. W. Plummer, the books for girls by C. W. Rankin and also by M. A. Taggart, in addition to many individual volumes of general appeal to children.

As in the 1890's, Holt ran into difficulties with some of his successful novelists when he refused to meet competitive bids stipulated by agents. In writing to James Pinker, representing the Williamsons, he pointed out that the success of THE LIGHTNING CONDUCTOR was attributable to the last chapter which the authors had added at his suggestion; that he had paid the authors $1,500 for the serial rights to THE PRINCESS PASSES without being able to sell them to a periodical.

He continued:

I think I am through making specified terms for books I have not seen, and probably through with buying periodical rights I cannot see a definite place for. It is unquestionably to your immediate interest at least, to scatter around your clients' books. If your conscience satisfies you that it is also to theirs—especially when it involves trusting them to publishers who do both these foolish things, don't wait for me.

Pinker didn't and the McClure and Doubleday firms published the subsequent novels written by the Williamsons.

Writing to George Meredith of Constable in January, 1908, Holt complained in reference to May Sinclair, "No literary agent, I am beginning to conclude . . . is going to keep an author to one publisher if he can help it. There were no commissions for him on what she did thru you and thru me."

Holt's interest in H. G. Wells began with his publication of the minor classic, THE TIME MACHINE, in 1895. Although the volume sold only 1,173 copies in seven years, Holt continued to express interest in Wells's writing. In 1903, Pinker informed him that Wells was looking for a publisher with whom he "can settle down in the comfortable assurance that each book as it comes along will be handled with skill and enterprise, and with due regard to its place in the general scheme of his work." Holt replied:

It would of course be my preference to have my heart in an author's books, and to have the terms fixed for the author's entire interests instead of turning on the simple question of how much each side can squeeze out of the other or withhold from the other, on each particular book; and I should be glad of any arrangement that will enable me to undertake Mr. Wells's books with that preference plainly realizable.

He offered his highest royalties: 10 per cent on the first 5,000 copies, 12½ on the next 2,500 copies, and 20 per cent on all sales thereafter. That, however, was acceptable to neither Wells nor Pinker. Years later, critical of MR. BRITLING, Holt wrote to Stuart P. Sherman that he was glad not to be Wells's publisher:

The object of this letter is to say that I have nearly finished MR. BRITLING, and that I find a good deal to admire in Mr. Wells, the details of which you understand a great deal better than I do, but that even in this book I find him rotten at the core, as he tries to make a substantial man out of one to whom he attributes half a dozen love affairs while married to a decent wife.

This rottenness of course stuck out huge in ANN VERONICA, and I suppose in lots more of his stuff I haven't read and haven't wanted to.

Quite a different situation obtained with the novels of William De Morgan, who had begun writing fiction in his sixties. William Heinemann was his publisher in England and, knowing Holt's ability to publish serious novels successfully, he gave him first refusal on JOSEPH VANCE. Holt readily accepted it, and it sold only moderately well until Fred G. Melcher, then a clerk at Lauriat's bookstore in Boston, began to promote it enthusiastically to his customers. Out of the 2,600 copies sold during the first year, Melcher alone sold 700, thus starting it on its popular career to a total of 40,000 copies. Before long a number of American publishers approached the elderly author. In August, 1907, Heinemann wrote to Holt: "He is being besieged by practically every house in America,—that is a fact,—the most respectable and highest standing among them. The offers come direct and come from agents, and he showed me a few days ago an offer of $4,000 if he would write a story of 40,000 words."

Holt replied, "I should be very surprised to learn that the Century Company, Scribner, Putnam, or Houghton Mifflin and Co. had been after De Morgan. If any of them has, pray give me particulars." On learning that Century and other publishers had offered De Morgan a royalty of 25 per cent, he told Heinemann what his terms would be: "The best contract (for the author, not for me) that I ever made was for 15% up to 5000, and 20% thereafter. That contract I shall never exceed." He added a week later that "if a novel goes to 30,000 for the first year, I will pay 5% more on the first 5000." He was also ready to pay De Morgan monthly royalties during the first six months after publication. Because Heinemann was both sensitive and sensible, and deprecated "plunging" and agents as much as Holt, he saw to it that De Morgan remained with Holt. And although none of the other De Morgan novels achieved the popularity of JOSEPH VANCE, all were promoted effectively over the years—to the mutual benefit of both author and publisher.

Another English publisher on very friendly terms with Holt was Sir Frederick Macmillan, with whom he carried on a personal correspondence for many years. Macmillan gave Holt first chance on a number of books, among them Bergson's CREATIVE EVOLUTION.

Holt was more interested in planning series of books than in single volumes. In 1901 he tried to interest Owen Wister in writing a series of brief popular biographies of leading Americans from Benjamin Franklin to General Sherman.

What a stunning thing you could make of it, if you did it as carefully and patiently as you must have done your Grant. It would establish you at once, I think, on the relatively permanent basis of history. . . . It seems a little like putting a racer in a cart, or a bird of paradise to brood over hen's eggs, to suggest to a fellow of your lovely frisky fancy to buckle down to this sort of prosaic work; but there are at least two things to be said about that. The work need not be prosaic, any more than James's PSYCHOLOGY is, or as much; and (seriously as aforesaid), the time when fancy ceaseth to be frisky, draweth nigh, and in this sober work she would probably find all the space for the light fantastic she would crave.

Wister, however, had other plans and begged off.

For several years Holt tried to arrange with J. M. Dent of England for the joint publication of a series of standard historical novels with settings ranging from ancient times to the end of the nineteenth century. Their correspondence was lengthy and detailed. In one letter Holt listed 121 novels to be considered. "No matter how valuable the books may be from a psychological or literary standpoint," he explained, "if they are not *interesting*, no chances must be taken before the success of the series is determined." Difficulties of copyright and reprinting arrangements, as well as a number of technical and financial complications, in the end caused both men to lose interest in the project.

This failure of Holt and Dent to reach a meeting of minds was very likely responsible for their lack of agreement on the American edition of Everyman's Library, which Dent was then evolving. Attracted as Holt was to the project, both he and Bristol, without the benefit of hindsight, considered Dent's terms entirely exorbitant. Since Dent refused to bargain, Holt relinquished what subsequently became one of the most profitable reprint series on the market.

Holt was more successful in developing his American Nature Series. In announcing it in 1906, he expressed the hope that it would "answer questions—those (outside the domain of philosophy) which the contemplation of Nature is constantly arousing in the mind of the unscientific intelligent person." It took him nearly two years of effort before he found suitable authors—eighteen in all—though not all actually produced. He tried to persuade G. F. Atkinson, who was completing his book on mushrooms, to let him list the volume in the series. "It would do the Series good, and the Series would do the book good—keep it permanently before the public." Atkinson, however, would not agree and Holt issued it separately. He also tried to interest Simon Newcomb in prepar-

106 ing a volume on the stars. "Now if the Star book in the Nature Series were to hit as well as the Chemistry or the Physiology and the Psychology and some other books in the Science Series, it would pay you mighty well to do it. The authors of some of these books have been raking in thousands a year for a good many years." Newcomb, however, had prior commitments and could not oblige.

Two other of his authors were more co-operative. President David Starr Jordan of Stanford, whose comprehensive and authoritative work, FISHES, Holt was about to publish, agreed to do a popular volume on the same subject. In February, 1903, he wrote, "I am willing to write any kind of a book in which I have the greatest interest, because it contains all the generalizations which an experience of nearly thirty years in fish work has enabled me to make." Vernon L. Kellogg, whose highly detailed study, AMERICAN INSECTS, was also on the Holt list, undertook to condense his book for the series. In time the series contained sixteen volumes.

In 1906, Holt also arranged to publish the American Public Problems Series, edited by R. C. Ringwalt. Its first volume was Bennett F. Hall's IMMIGRATION AND ITS EFFECT UPON THE UNITED STATES. For various reasons the series became inactive very soon thereafter. Holt's persistent interest in brief biographies of leading Americans led him to contract with John Erskine to edit LEADING AMERICAN NOVELISTS, with R. M. Johnson to prepare LEADING AMERICAN ESSAYISTS, and with D. S. Jordan to edit LEADING AMERICAN SCIENTISTS. Holt also negotiated with William Ellery Leonard for a volume on religious leaders, but nothing came of it.

One of Holt's memorable ventures was THE HOME BOOK OF VERSE, compiled and edited by B. E. Stevenson. The work had its inception as early as 1900. Stevenson, lunching with Holt, mentioned his interest in preparing such a volume and Holt encouraged him. Their first idea was an anthology not to exceed 1,000 two-column pages and to sell for $3.00. Holt's terms of 10-per-cent royalty were at Stevenson's urging increased to 12½ per cent if the book sold 10,000 in ten years and to 15 per cent if that sale were made in five years. Wishing to assure the success of the book, Holt suggested Henry Van Dyke as collaborator, but Stevenson preferred to do it alone.

The compilation advanced slowly, and its scope broadened considerably in the process. Stevenson, a small-town librarian, energetic and ingenious, wrote mysteries to supplement his salary. It was his hope to earn enough money from his fiction to enable him to give more time to the anthology. THE HOLLADAY CASE, which Holt published, sold well enough to attract the attention of other publishers. When Stevenson informed Holt that Frank H. Dodd had made him a tempting offer for his next book, Holt replied, "I think Dodd is a good fellow, but he was apparently brought up with ideas different from mine, of what we then used to call professional decency; and you know my notions about the desirability of an author keeping his books together." Stevenson remained with him for a while longer, but when Holt would not meet a new attractive offer from an agent for Dodd, Stevenson decided to leave him.

Their relations remained friendly and their correspondence concerning the anthology was copious and complex. When Stevenson sought to lessen his permission costs by omitting certain poems, Holt urged him to retain them. The completed manuscript was finally ready late in 1911. The estimated cost of manufacture was so great that Holt, often the pessimist, feared financial loss and considered giving up the project. "The day when THE HOME BOOK OF VERSE was published I would have sold out of it for twenty-five cents on the dollar." Issued in eight volumes that included 3,500 poems and extended to 3,800 pages, the work was priced at $8.00. Stevenson dedicated it to Holt.

The success of the book was immediate. Somewhat later Holt brought out one-volume and two-volume editions, and for a half century the book has continued to be a staple item on the Holt list. In 1915 Stevenson edited THE HOME BOOK OF VERSE FOR YOUNG FOLKS, and ten years later THE HOME BOOK OF MODERN VERSE. Both volumes did well. Later, with Henry Holt dead, Bristol declined to contract for Stevenson's collection of classic and modern quotations, and Dodd, Mead brought it out to that firm's considerable profit.

Holt's letters to authors abound with sage advice or realistic comment, but they also reveal his rooted prejudices and sober pessimism. Writing to Arthur Steadman about his novel, he stated that "the last chapter of a book is apt to be the most important chapter," and an author who does not realize that "stands, in my mind, a mighty poor chance of writing a good novel." He told Lincoln Steffens that his manuscript of short stories would have a poor sale because slum stories were not popular. To Charles Francis Adams he stated that there was no demand for a new edition of CHAPTERS OF ERIE, but that there was a need for a book on leading railroad men. "You have more of the data within reach, probably than any other literary man, and I wouldn't be surprised if you could get some fun out of it. You certainly could make it of immense value as a history of railroad development." But Adams was not interested.

In 1903, Paul Reynolds offered Arnold Bennett's THE TRUTH ABOUT AN AUTHOR to Holt. Although Bennett had already published several novels, Holt refused the requested 15-per-cent royalty. He was eager to publish Grazia Deledda's work, and went to great trouble to persuade her to write an additional chapter to DOPO IL DIVERZIO for copyright purposes. He had an interchange of several letters with Max Nordau, the French thinker, concerning his DEGENERATION, in which he evidenced strong interest, but before he could make up his mind, Appleton contracted for it. To an author whose novel had been returned for revision Holt wrote, "I have lately awakened with a bang to a realization that all the time I have spent over American fiction during over forty years, has brought us just two books that paid a decent profit."

In 1909, he was favorably impressed with Professor Grant Showerman's essays, though he knew they would not repay costs. Informing him of this, he continued, "The stuff is good, and I'm going to print it. If I lose on it, I shall not care a continental. The chances of losing, however, are so good that I shall not attempt to pay you any royalty until I have at least got my money back." At the same time he refused Joseph Conrad's new novel in view of the poor sale of his previous books. He was ready to publish Ellen Glasgow's novels, but only "if she were to come of her own motion to me"; while he adhered to "courtesy," Doubleday did not and got her.

When Alice Duer Miller, whose novel had sold only 550 copies, asked for an advance on her new work, Holt considered the request "damned nonsense," although he offered to publish it on his usual terms. He admitted, however, that she could no doubt find a publisher who would give her the advance. "There are fools enough in the publishing trade now to do anything, probably more than ever before, which is saying a great deal."

A favored author of Holt's was Frank Jewett Mather. This Princeton teacher of art had a book of essays on collectors. It had been rejected by several publishers before he submitted it to Holt with a letter relating his experience. Holt liked the essays and told Mather that the publishers were probably right about the volume's limited appeal, "but that ought not to have deterred them from publishing the book. I shall consider it a pleasure and an honor to do so. . . . All this is on the supposition that you are not one of the authors who take it for granted that a publisher is a Pactolean spring whence money comes whether he makes it or not." He offered no royalties on the first 1,500 copies, 20 per cent on the next 1,500 copies, and 15 per cent thereafter. "Don't be too confident, however, that we will ever get there."

Although Holt had the reputation of being illiberal to authors, he never took undue advantage of them. As a sound businessman, he wanted first to assure himself against loss before paying royalties, especially on books by new authors. Once his costs were repaid, he more than made up in additional royalties. An interesting, if exceptional instance was the royalty arrangement in 1909 with Professor George E. Russell for his HYDRAULICS. No royalty was paid on the first 700 copies sold—"this exception being made to cover the publisher's initial outlay for typesetting, electrotyping, reproduction of illustrations, and incidental expenses chargeable solely to the book." Thereafter Holt agreed to pay 15 per cent of list "on the annual sales of 500 copies or less," and another 2 per cent on every additional 100 copies sold annually, rising to 25 per cent "on a sale above 900 copies." Since the book proved relatively successful and long-lasting, Russell received the maximum royalty over many years.

IX. Henry Holt and Alfred Harcourt

In 1910, having reached the age of seventy, Holt told his "assistants": "In a few years you'll have to get along without me, and you may as well begin practicing. I'm not coming to the office any more." This statement notwithstanding, he remained the real head of the firm for years thereafter. And while he absented himself from the office for greater periods, he insisted on being consulted on every move of importance. His prime interest was in the trade department, of which he had that year made Alfred Harcourt the manager; his letters of instruction and indoctrination make a lively text for the education of a potential publisher.

On their graduation from Columbia in 1904, Harcourt and Donald Brace were both employed by Holt—Harcourt to edit and sell books and Brace, who was interested in typography, to help in their manufacture. Harcourt made long seasonal trips to the larger cities in the East and Middle West. He found Holt a firm disciplinarian, favoring high ideals, but no longer as hospitable to new ideas as he once was. "But when the new idea was really good," Harcourt recalled years later, "he let me go my way, sometimes with modifications." He persuaded Holt in 1910 to let him go to London to seek new manuscripts and to strengthen contact with British publishers.

Although Harcourt was the formal head of the trade department, Holt watched him like a mother hen. While at Burlington he wrote to him frequently and guided his actions with a firm hand. With an old man's arrogated privilege, he expatiated on matters in order to spur or slacken the young man's enthusiasms. Their correspondence reveals the valuable training Harcourt received before he embarked on his own distinguished career.

As early as 1905 when Harcourt, the ambitious neophyte, suggested that the firm sell Champlin's CYCLOPEDIA FOR YOUNG FOLKS by

112   mail on a subscription basis, Holt told him, "The more I think of it, the more shaky I am about going into the installment subscription business. It will require a good deal of machinery and expense, and it is the sort of thing I detest from the bottom of my soul." In 1909, ready to put Harcourt in charge of trade books, Holt tried to encourage his initiative. "It gives me the creeps to realize how large a factor in our year's business a single author like De Morgan is. The only way to get the factor of less terrifying proportions is to get more such authors."

Holt, unlike Harcourt, believed that publishers do too much traveling and said that he "had no fancy for having canvassers going to bore people in my name." When Harcourt continued to urge the employment of an additional salesman, Holt wrote: "I incline to think that it is more important to work at getting books than it is to work at selling them. I think the right ones come mighty close to selling themselves." It was only in 1911 that Holt acquiesced in the employment of August H. Gehrs as a trade salesman. The same situation obtained in the textbook field, and Bristol complained that books can no longer be sold without travelers. "We have fewer in proportion to our sales," he told Holt, "I think, than any other education house," and added that he lost the Indiana state adoption because no Holt representative had visited its schools for three years.

In 1909, Holt sent Harcourt to Ida Tarbell to ascertain whether he could approach Jane Addams about her autobiography without poaching on other publishers, and incidentally to ask Miss Tarbell if her next book was free. "If you don't find her, don't write to her. Letters are the devil, as you will find out some day to your cost, if I don't prevent your finding out—every man must, unless prevented."

Harcourt had read and liked SISTER CARRIE, but Holt vetoed his proposal to publish Dreiser. Harcourt also sent him a copy of Bennett's OLD WIVES' TALE. Having read it, Holt wrote: "There is certainly a great deal of merit in it. It is the queerest book I ever saw. I cannot see where the popularity is to come from." The next day he added, "The more I think of OLD WIVES' TALE the more I cannot get it out of my head. What is there to make it popular except its vividness and its vivid presentation of uninteresting things and people?"

Holt was troubled by the small sale of new novels. Years back, he told Harcourt, "the Harpers could sell enough of any book that was fit to publish to make it pay; and I suspect Appleton could; and even a little concern like mine could come about three times as near to it as it can now." Referring to some of the firm's unsuccessful fiction, he declared, "Lord what nonsense all this miscellaneous publication is beside such books as Hazen's History and Salisbury's Physiographies! The fact of the matter is that the great Bobbs-Merrill epoch drove people crazy, and they have not yet quite recovered."

Although he discouraged Harcourt from considering middling novels, Holt became quite excited when a good one came along. When Heinemann submitted JEAN CHRISTOPHE to him, he read it with increasing enthusiasm and told Harcourt to inform Heinemann of its acceptance. "Tell him and everybody else that I am the boy to send great literature to for its appreciation, also that I am the boy to do the warning off from a public too stupid to appreciate it."

When Harcourt went to England in 1910, Holt advised him in detail on every project that came up for consideration. Most important of the ventures Harcourt favored was the People's University Library, a series to be launched by Williams and Norgate under the editorship of Gilbert Murray, Herbert Fisher, and J. Arthur Thomson. Holt's response was prompt and discouraging:

114   You realize of course that it is not at all on all-fours with Everyman's Library. There is a wide and existing demand for every book in Everyman's, with the exception of a few perhaps in the selection of which they were a little too catholic. Virtually there is not one book in that Library which is an experiment.

On the other hand, nearly every book in the People's University Library will be an experiment, as nearly every new book is.

I should not care to undertake it at all unless every book for this side should pass through the hands of an American editor, and what we would get in that process I don't know! . . .

There is no way of being sure that people will write what they are told to, or what they ought to. . . . There are a thousand ways for a book to go wrong, where there is only one for it to go right.

Yet Holt did not want to let the series go the way Everyman's had gone. The next week he wrote: "Everyman's was offered to us on terms which I don't remember, but which Bristol says, even in view of its present apparent success, were preposterous; and he has no doubt that it subsequently went to Dutton on much better terms. That is not an infrequent experience in our gambling business." Several days later he again wrote to Harcourt: "I have been asking myself very seriously whether I have been too much of a bear on the W. & N. Library scheme, but I am satisfied that on the whole I am correct." Nevertheless he told Harcourt not to let Williams and Norgate give the People's University Library to "one of the mushroom houses" in America before letting him meet their terms.

Negotiations continued for months. Harcourt again went to London in October, determined to take the Home University Library, as it was now called. But Holt still hesitated.

The most I shall do is to try to take a position where I can handle any books in it that are worth handling and let the rest go. Those in it that are worth handling may possibly be one in five, more probably one in ten. . . . You have been set on fire by Williams & Norgate's enthusiasm, and their enthusiasm is simply made, as mine often was before I learned better, by the bigness of a scheme—that won't work.

He finally accepted the series when Williams and Norgate consented to accept an American editor to include books originating in the United States, and to permit Holt to publish only those volumes for which he thought there was an American market. "Now that you boys have got that Williams & Norgate series," he told Harcourt, "I am going to take as cheerful a view of it as I can. I'd rather see young people take a foolish thing than turn down a good one."

Williams and Norgate published the first eleven volumes of the Home University Library in April, 1911. The books sold well and, by November, Harcourt was informed that "we have already considerably passed 300,000 of sales." Holt announced the series in a April issue of PUB-LISHERS' WEEKLY: "This series aims to supply the need of laymen and students for readable *new* books, inspired by knowledge of the latest research and critical thought, comprehensively planned rather for advanced than juvenile readers." The books sold unevenly, and those adapted to college use did best. In 1912, to stimulate sales, the original price of 75 cents was reduced to 50 cents, but that helped little. Holt pointed out that "its circulation here is virtually restricted to the highly educated. The rank and file of American readers have their tastes formed and supplied by the Sunday newspapers and the cheap periodicals. The idea of gathering a library of cheap books on substantial subjects is virtually unknown among them."

When Thornton Butterworth took over the series from Williams and Norgate in the 1920's, he complained that Holt was not promoting it aggressively enough. He urged a more energetic American editor and more attractive designs. An accounting made in 1930 showed that the American sales had reached their peak in 1915 with a total of 33,310 copies, had sunk to a low of 12,449 in 1921, and had risen to a relative average of 17,571 in 1929. The low sale in the 1920's was especially bad in view of the increased number of volumes in the series. In 1942 the series was given up without regret.

An interesting administrative procedure was the formation of the "senate" when Henry Holt began to absent himself from the office for long periods of time. Its members were the several executives who met periodically to discuss book projects and other pertinent matters before making their reports to Holt. Usually Roland Holt sent his father frequent memos on the senate's recommendations. When Harcourt went abroad, he advised the senate of his activities in addition to writing to Holt. In January, 1911, he rejected George Moore's HAIL AND FAREWELL, explaining to the senate: "It's certainly immoral. On the whole I rather feel it would hardly be fair to our other authors to put his name alongside theirs." Holt was not even told of this strait-laced decision.

In June, 1911, Holt, still worried about the effect of his pessimism on Harcourt, wrote to him, "Now when I do this bearish talk about the miscellaneous business, don't think that I fail to appreciate you. You have done very well, but you have had scant time, and a mighty desert field." A little later he again wrote, "The slogan of the office to me delivered through Roland, has long been 'Don't discourage Harcourt.' A proper slogan would be: 'Help Harcourt into some activity worthy of his abilities.' " He also advised him never to let a prospective author say no "because he is apt to stick to it," and "good authors were always busy

and likely to say no; he should be told to think about it and be visited
later for his answer."

When sales figures that year did not yield the expected profit, Holt told Harcourt, "It is time for some pretty hard head-scratching somewhere. Any fool can spend more money than the other fellow. The wise man is he who accomplishes the same results by spending less." The next week he wrote that he realized that in times past "there was not quite as mean a fight over every author that comes above the surface, as there now is by any common set of curs over a bone. . . . I don't regret any of the 'standing alone' that I have done in regard to the absurdities of the trade."

Holt was pleased to publish Bergson's CREATIVE EVOLUTION because it was highly praised by men he respected. He himself could make little of Bergson's ideas and in 1912 confided to Harcourt: "I should even question my honesty in publishing Bergson, if it were not that he seems to make a considerable intellectual stir among people who probably would not be capable of making any stir without such brilliant phrases as his to attract them." He wrote again three days later that an article on Bergson in the DIAL "has opened my eyes to something well worth while. Bergson will help people see the beautiful side of Evolution." When Bergson came to New York to lecture at Columbia, Holt asked Harcourt to find out about the kind of person Bergson was before he invited him to his house, for he would do so only "if he is a gentleman." Harcourt ascertained that Bergson was a gentleman and the invitation was sent.

In 1913, Holt was annoyed when Harcourt bought 750 sheets of Fielding Hall's THE WORLD SOUL. Himself hard at work on his massive COSMIC RELATIONS, he considered the Hall book unworthy of his imprint and was ready to scrap the sheets and take his loss. When Har-

118   court objected, Holt wrote: "We can't afford to put out a humbug book for the sake of getting our money back." The next day he wrote again: "I shall never be satisfied at having my name on the book . . . but in future, I guess all books in philosophy, religion and science had better come before the oldest member of the house who happens to be alive—you may be that some day."

Harcourt's education continued through the decade. By letter and in person Holt gave him the benefit of his long experience and ripe wisdom —including the accrued prejudices of nearly a half century. Harcourt was an apt pupil; he absorbed the good and relegated the rest to his own activities in later years. Under his own aegis, but always with Holt's advice and approval, appeared a number of books that added luster to an already fine list. In addition to Romain Rolland and Bergson, he brought out books by such distinguished scientists and scholars as Lovat Frazer, J. Arthur Thomson, John Dewey, Edwin B. Holt, and Henri Lichtenberger. Among the novelists were Rose Macaulay, Dorothy Canfield Fisher, Julien Benda, C. E. Montague, Martin Anderson Nexö, Henry Handel Richardson, and Romer Wilson. A strong part of the list was the poetry of Robert Frost, Walter de la Mare, Carl Sandburg, Louis Untermeyer, Sarah N. Cleghorn, Padraic Colum, and John Crowe Ransom. Plays and books on drama were acquired mostly by Roland Holt.

Although Henry Holt delegated much of the work on trade books to Harcourt, he continued to correspond directly with a number of authors and to read the manuscripts Harcourt considered publishable. One of these authors was Mrs. Fisher, who was brought to the firm by Harcourt. As early as 1911, when a rival publisher made her an offer, she informed Harcourt, "I've taken a copy of the man's name and address to write him my old formula of 'no thank you sir. I'm engaged to Mr. Holt.' " In 1915 she wrote to him from Vermont: "Who should suddenly

drop in yesterday for a two-minute call but Mr. Holt himself. . . . I
found the same astonishing fondness for the old gentleman spring up at
the sight of him. . . . I do love to see him."

Shortly thereafter Holt was given her manuscript of THE BENT
TWIG. He read it with his usual critical care and wrote her:

It is a good book, but seems to be encrusted with rather more
superfluous matter than equally good books often are. . . . Nothing
superfluous is ever good, especially in a work of art. In fact I have
had beauty defined as freedom from superfluity. It looks to me as if
when your pen got to going with things with which you were very
familiar, you yielded pretty freely to the pleasure of letting go. I
think the book would greatly gain by filing and sandpapering off
from, perhaps, a fifth to a quarter. . . . I think that the writer of a
book ought to look at every sentence, every word with the question:
Can I do equally well without this?

Unlike Mrs. Voynich, Mrs. Fisher reacted most gratefully:

I pity you with all my heart if you have never known the exciting
pleasure you have just given me, if you have never had the electrifying
experience which has just ended for me with the last page of the
proofs! It's been one of the dreams of my life, to have just such a
criticism as that, illuminating, full, precise, and accurate as a surgeon's
scalpel. . . . Blessings on your keen eye.

In 1915, Harcourt, with Holt's approval, arranged for the American
publication of Makers of the Nineteenth Century, a series edited by
Basil Williams. Among the volumes included were Sir Edward Cook's

120 JOHN DELANE OF THE TIMES, Lord Charnwood's ABRAHAM
LINCOLN, H. S. Elliott's HERBERT SPENCER, Basil Williams'
CECIL RHODES, Madame Duclaux's VICTOR HUGO, J. J. Ham-
mond's LORD SHAFTSBURY, F. O. Maurice's GENERAL LEE, and
W. M. Salter's NIETZSCHE, THE THINKER. Harcourt also published
Walter Lippmann's STAKES OF DIPLOMACY and took over his two
earlier books. At Louis Untermeyer's recommendation he brought out
Walter de la Mare's THE LISTENERS. Variety and distinction were
added to the Holt list during this period by such books as Simeon
Strunsky's BALSHAZZAR'S COURT and other volumes of essays, Lil-
lian Wald's THE HOUSE ON HENRY STREET, Caspar S. Yost's
PATIENCE WORTH, Thomas Burke's NIGHTS IN LONDON, Sir Ar-
thur Quiller Couch's THE WORKMANSHIP OF SHAKESPEARE, Joel
Spingarn's CREATIVE CRITICISM, and Stuart P. Sherman's ON
CONTEMPORARY CRITICISM.

The consideration of Sherman's volume of essays provided Harcourt
with one of Holt's important lessons. In May, 1917, Sherman submitted
his manuscript to Holt. After a careful reading Holt sent it to Harcourt,
stating: "Paul More and Mather probably call this man the first critic in
America. I don't think we can afford to let him go elsewhere. . . . Write
me what you and the Senate think." Harcourt favored rejecting the
manuscript because of its limited market. Holt's response was in keeping
with his lifelong philosophy of publishing:

When I sent you Stuart Sherman's MS. I was entirely ready to lose
whatever it will cost to publish it, unless you should find in it something loudly calling for modification and he would be unwilling to
make the modification. There being nothing of that kind, I want you
to go ahead with it. He is by common consent the first literary critic

in America, and it is worth our while to lose some time, tissue and
money on him, for the sake of the luster he'll cast on our list.

The contract sent to Sherman exempted the first 1,000 copies from
royalties, with double the usual royalties on the second 1,000. In a talk
at this time Holt admitted that he was ready to lose money on a good
trade book because of his profits on textbooks.

That Holt's prejudices seldom blinded him to merit in a manuscript
was evidenced in connection with Spingarn. It was understandable that
Holt should favor Sherman, since their critical standards were similar.
Spingarn, however, was an impressionistic critic, with views contrary to
those favored by Holt. Yet Holt recognized Spingarn's scholarship and
acute perceptions and offered him 15 per cent of list for CREATIVE
CRITICISM. Published in the same year as Sherman's book, it stirred up
a good deal of controversy and its influence was long felt in academic
circles. After four years, however, it had sold only 908 copies.

In 1918, Harcourt, whose salary and commission had averaged $10,-
000 a year shortly before the war, but had shrunken considerably with
the decline in sales, received an offer from George H. Doran of $10,-
000 a year in salary plus a commission on sales. In need of a larger
income and aware that Holt would not meet the offer at this time, he
wrote to him frankly: "I'd much rather stay with H. H. & Co., but I
have financial responsibilities since my father died land poor, which
won't permit my being quixotic in the face of this proposal." He suggested that he would be "willing to split the difference for the sake of
my happiness here and my future here," and intimated that he would
accept a salary of $750 a month.

Three days later Harcourt telegraphed Holt: "After week-end reflection I feel my roots are too deep in this business to be pulled out by

dazzling schemes or immediate income. Please forget my letter unless it or anything else has disturbed you about my future here. Please wire me on this point." Holt's telegraphic reply stated: "Am glad and proud of your decision, and hope and believe you will not regret it." In a letter he wrote: "I hope I can safely say that I never made money a controlling motive. Probably you know cases where I disregarded it utterly, and yet through an exceptionally long life I have had a reasonable amount of it, until this war pinch came."

All went well that summer and fall. In August Holt asked Harcourt to secure a small edition of Lytton Strachey's EMINENT VICTORIANS, but nothing came of it. Harcourt at that time reassured Holt of his positive interest in the UNPARTIZAN REVIEW, published by the firm. With the conclusion of the armistice in November, he lost no time in going to England in order to get first chance at books written during the war. He found London dreary but exciting. Among the books he bought was Bertrand Russell's ROADS TO FREEDOM, which dealt with the radical forces then agitating the world. The conservative WESTMINSTER GAZETTE had commended it as "good medicine for these times for those who have the courage to look facts in the face."

On his return to New York he was dismayed to learn that the book had been rejected by cable, Holt and the senate agreeing that such a book was unworthy of the firm's imprint. Reminiscing years later, Harcourt stated: "That I could consider anything by Bertrand Russell was bad enough, but that I could even read a book that mentioned bolshevism with anything but contempt was either treachery or aberration." In fact he exaggerated Holt's repugnance to "dangerous doctrine." Although Holt was loath to have such a book on his list, Harcourt himself stated that Holt's "high business principles made him suffer at the thought of going back on a bargain." The volume was published with

the amended title of PROPOSED ROADS TO FREEDOM and sold
surprisingly well. Ironically, when Russell was asked by the firm nineteen
years later to revise the work, he refused on the ground "that necessary
alterations would be so great that hardly a page of the old book could
stand as it is."

The experience jolted Harcourt. He assumed "that Henry Holt would
never feel safe with me again." Repressed thoughts of resigning and
starting his own firm now emerged full-fledged. Informing Christopher
Morley that he was leaving Holt, he wrote: "There was no acute cause
for my decision, but it was the ripening of doubts about my future here
which had been forming for some months." Robert Frost, congratulating
him on July 4, 1919, on forming his own business, continued: "I suppose I should be more excited if I hadn't been looking for it to happen
ever since something you said to me somewhere in a narrow side street
as we walked across town to lunch two or three years ago." Later Harcourt stretched the truth to the point of asserting that Holt had been
training his younger sons "to carry on the business in the way in which
he believed," when in fact neither of them had any connection with
either publishing or the firm until Harcourt had left. The parting on May
8 was friendly. Holt appreciated his abilities and ambitions, and Harcourt had this to say of his employer years later: "I always cared for
him, and I know that the fifteen years I had with him, at first absorbing
his ideas, then developing my own, gave me invaluable training, even
when I was struggling with what seemed unreasonable conservatism.
Nothing 'half-baked' or shoddy could get by Henry Holt."

Once Harcourt's resignation became known, several publishers approached him with offers. It was rumored that he was tendered the presidency of Harper and Brothers. In August, Bristol informed Holt: "Knopf
offered Harcourt a partnership after he resigned, and Harcourt made a

definite counter-proposal, which included becoming a senior partner, with Knopf's rich father as a silent partner to the tune of $100,000. The Knopfs didn't see it."

In the June 28, 1919, issue of PUBLISHERS' WEEKLY an editorial commented on the decline of families in publishing. Obviously inspired by Harcourt's talk with his friend Fred Melcher, it stated that Henry Holt's sons were taking control of the firm. "The one drawback to business enterprises in which the law of family succession prevails is that less opportunity is afforded to younger men who came from outside family ranks into the business, no matter how valuable they may become." Harcourt was praised as one of "the most appreciated and effective men in the trade" and gratification was expressed at the amicable separation. "In fact, some of the authors whose association with the elder house have in these later years been through Mr. Harcourt, will be transferred in a friendly spirit to the new firm."

Actually, Bristol's attitude was hardly friendly. Having borrowed money to buy the Holt stock owned by Harcourt and Brace and having long been the managing head of the old firm, he resented the tenor of the editorial and even more Harcourt's raiding of Holt authors. In a letter to Holt he asserted that the content of the editorial was instigated by Harcourt, and added: "I can see no fairness in our denuding ourselves of books which we paid him to get and to sell—at least not until we feel moved to do so. . . . Any such wholesale disposal (if you can call it wholesale) as Harcourt is trying to bring about is a decided departure for a going concern."

Holt agreed and sent him his reply to the editorial. With certain changes accepted by Holt, the letter denied that the firm was a family concern and stated that Roland Holt, the only son in the firm, "never professed to be a business man, though he has done good service in

literary matters and correspondence." Holt further explained that E. N.
Bristol, the firm's "chief director since I retired from active business
nearly ten years ago . . . the ablest man the house ever had, and whose
modesty leads him to object to my even giving his name here, expects
to remain with it during the rest of his business career." Furthermore,
"no significant change will be made in the general management by the
withdrawal of Mr. Harcourt, who has been a director only three years.
The article also appears to carry an intimation that we have handed
over to Mr. Harcourt in mass, to begin business with, a lot of authors.
Our innocence and our generosity have not gone that far."

Several days later Bristol reported to Holt that the authors Harcourt
had taken away should not do irreparable damage to the trade department. "Mrs. Fisher and Frost (if Frost) and possibly Untermeyer are
all that count."

Apparently he was not concerned about Carl Sandburg and Walter
Lippmann, to mention only two others he must have known about. Of
Sinclair Lewis he did not know enough to take cognizance, although he
was to be the most profitable of the departing authors.

As early as February, 1916, Lewis had promised Harcourt to give
his next novel to Holt. At that time he had written to Harper, the
publisher of his first novels:

Doran was ready to guarantee me a sale of 10,000 on THE HAWK,
and that far more reliable firm—a firm without any of the earmarks
of Bobbs Merrill or other author-snatchers—Henry Holt Co., were
ready to guarantee me a sale of 20,000 on HAWK. . . . In the light
of these preferred guarantees I can't help being sorrowful over 3665,
even though I'm aware that that must be equal to, or even greater
than, the average sale of a second novel.

In his next undated letter to Harcourt, Lewis wrote: "I betcha I *do* do MAIN ST. before another year is over." In reply on April 4, 1917, Harcourt assured him that if his "former publishers do not publish THE INNOCENTS, we are ready to take over your contract with them." He implied that in any event Holt was to bring out the next novel. "As your plans now shape themselves, this will be the novel about which we have talked as entitled MAIN STREET." He proposed a royalty of 15 per cent on the first 10,000 copies, 17½ per cent on the next 10,000, and 20 per cent thereafter. He also promised a generous advance and intensive advertising. That September, Lewis informed Harcourt's secretary that "the novel, the great and only presumably-to-be-issued by Holt novel, is going strong. I've written 80,000 words. Looks as though it would be about 130,000 words in all."

Negotiations dragged, owing to Harper's obstruction. Finally on February 28, 1919, Lewis sent Holt a signed copy of the contract for MAIN STREET. Meantime he was making an automobile tour across the United States and describing it in articles for THE SATURDAY EVENING POST. When he intimated to Harcourt that this material should be issued in a book entitled FREE AIR, the latter replied on April 10 to urge postponement. "I'd like to have you put your best foot forward, especially on the first step with us, and have a book the whole organization will be crazy about and that will justify all the fuss we want to make over the first book you publish with us: in short, MAIN STREET."

When Harcourt left Holt a month later, he wanted Lewis to get a release from his contract with Holt for MAIN STREET. He therefore advised him to write not to Bristol but to Roland Holt, and this Lewis did on June 16:

Despite my long and hearty respect for the Company and my per-

sonal liking for you and others, yet after all Harcourt has always
been the man in the firm whom I have best known and with whom I
have done business, as book-reviewer and fellow publisher and author,
and while I don't know what his plans are, I want to be loyal to him
and stick by him.

Lewis of course knew what Harcourt's plans were, but this misstate-
ment would not have mattered to the gentle and ingenuous Roland. Like
his father, he would not keep an author against his will; without troubling
to consult with Bristol, he returned the canceled contract to Lewis with
his good wishes.

X. A Transitional Period: 1919-1926

In the course of a short time Henry Holt and Company lost a major part of its key personnel. Harcourt had taken with him not only Brace, who headed the production department, but Gehrs (sales manager), and Ellen K. Aeyrs (his secretary and assistant). Maxwell Aley (promotion manager) left to go to another firm. In addition Joseph Vogelius, fifty-eight years with the firm and Holt's alter ego in the office, retired—he died less than a year later—and Ambrose Dearborn, Bristol's associate in the textbook department and Harcourt's successor as secretary of the company, died suddenly in September, 1920. It devolved upon Bristol to supervise every department, and he worked energetically to that end. Roland Holt considered him the firm's "tower of strength."

The octogenarian Henry Holt regarded the depletion of personnel with philosophical optimism. Ten years earlier he had written to E. Byrne Hackett, a prominent bookman: "The rewards of the book publishing business are so inadequate to its requirements that I am not attempting to influence my younger boys to go into it." In his GARRULITIES, however, he stated that the departure of Harcourt and Vogelius did not really matter, since "my boys were back from the war, and ready for the vacancies"—a highly unrealistic assertion.

With his youngest son Elliot, still in Europe after his release from the army, Holt wrote to Roland: "I shouldn't think of *sending* Elliot over now. But *as he is there now,* I think it worthwhile for him to do what I propose. Explain this to the Senate." Elliot thus made his first visit to English publishers. On his return he began to travel for the trade department. Meantime Bristol was glad to have Lincoln MacVeagh return to the trade division. He had been with it from 1915 until he joined the armed forces in 1917. Back from the army, he was vacationing in Vermont. Learning of Harcourt's resignation, he wrote to Bristol on June 17, 1919: "Perhaps you would like to have me come back, say after

the 4th, and do my small part to help along." On the seventh he returned
to the Holt office and began to attend to the daily routine of the department.

One of the first things MacVeagh did was to write to his friend Franklin D. Roosevelt, then Assistant Secretary of the Navy, to ask if he would prepare a book on the build-up of the Navy. Roosevelt informed him that he was planning to write two books on the Navy but was already committed to other publishers. Neither work had been written when he was struck down with infantile paralysis.

Roland Holt did his best to help, but he lacked executive ability. Writing to William Beebe on July 8, 1919, he complained: "For the last three weeks I have been so busy that life has scarcely been worth living, and have had no chance to write to you or other friends any human word." He assured him that the "miscellaneous department will become stronger than ever, and very much wish that we might have a book by you to honor our list." Although JUNGLE PEACE had sold over 8,000 copies in less than a year and was still selling well, Bebee's next book went to Putnam, whose sponsorship of his next research project made the transfer unavoidable.

With the momentum of the company continuing despite the disruptions, the year's business ended on a hopeful note. MacVeagh was made head of the trade department, Moore C. Tussey came from Macmillan to take charge of the college department upon Burnett's retirement, and Bristol's son, Herbert, was placed in the production department. Henry Holt, appreciative of Bristol's endeavors, offered him half of the year's profits that would have gone to Harcourt, but Bristol insisted that others in the firm share the commission with him. "The whole staff is exerting itself most loyally to make up for Harcourt's and Brace's defection—and under specially trying conditions."

130   One of MacVeagh's early achievements was to make a friend of Robert Frost. He was also instrumental in bringing Robert Benchley and Stephen Vincent Benét to Holt. The latter was a senior at Yale when MacVeagh read some of his poems and contracted to publish a volume of them— HEAVENS AND EARTH. He also accepted Benét's partly written novel, THE BEGINNING OF WISDOM. "I have read it," he wrote to the young author, "and enjoyed it, and am grateful to you for the chance. There are some pages I had no choice but to read over and over again for the beauty of the sentences. There is glorious writing in this book." Benét, pleased, replied that although other publishers had made him offers, he was glad to give the novel to Holt. This book and Benchley's OF ALL THINGS were published in 1921.

    MacVeagh went to England in 1920, and among the books he brought back were Albert Einstein's RELATIVITY and Marcel Proust's SWANN'S WAY. Highly interested in Proust, MacVeagh deplored the hesitancy of publishers to bring him before the American public: "I believe a publisher should make perfectly sure, within human limitations, that the public will not support the venture before deciding against publication of such a work." He also tried to get Bertrand Russell's new book—having been instructed by Holt that Russell was "worth holding on to" in view of his retraction of his "communistic faith"— but Stanley Unwin, Russell's publisher, informed MacVeagh that "in accordance with the author's wishes the first offer of the book will have to go to Mr. Alfred Harcourt, who you will remember was responsible for the publication of ROADS TO FREEDOM at a time when you had definitely cabled to us that you did not wish to be associated with the book." MacVeagh accepted Burke's new book but dropped him as the firm's scout in England—he having brought it practically nothing. He did not take Rolland's ABOVE THE BATTLE, which he considered an inferior

work, but assured the agent that Holt wanted to have first refusal on
Rolland's future writings.

Meantime the textbook department continued its profitable activity. One of the most successful text books ever published by Holt was Robert S. Woodworth's PSYCHOLOGY. Since Woodworth was considered one of the country's most prominent teachers of psychology around 1920, his text was sought by several textbook publishers. Harcourt, a former student of his, tried his utmost to acquire the manuscript. Arthur Burnett had long courted Woodworth and had persuaded him that Holt was the leading publisher in psychology. On March 24, 1920, he wrote to him: "If you are willing to negotiate with us at once, our terms (which you will of course consider confidential) are 15% of the net wholesale price of the book." Discovering that Harcourt had also offered Woodworth a contract and fearing that its terms might be better, he at once consulted with Bristol and informed Woodworth that he had inadvertently given him the wrong terms—having meant them to be 15 per cent of the retail price. Woodworth thereupon decided in Holt's favor.

Burnett had also arranged for the publication of Woodworth's EX-PERIMENTAL PSYCHOLOGY at "a royalty of 15% of the net whole-sale price of the book on all copies sold after enough copies have been exempted to pay for the cost of composition and electrotyping." More than eighteen years later, with PSYCHOLOGY an extraordinary success and with the prospects for the finally completed EXPERIMENTAL PSYCHOLOGY relatively favorable, T. J. Wilson, manager of the college department, made proper amends in a letter to Professor Woodworth:

Frankly, circumstances seem to have changed considerably and we all feel that this royalty clause is unfair to you. We don't think it at all right to exempt any copies from royalty with the first copy sold and would like, therefore, to make the following provisions apply, rather than those quoted above: 15% of wholesale and an additional 5% in any year the sale is 2500 or more.

We hope you will understand that our reason for making this change in your favor is because of our sincere pride in our publication of your books and our wish to remedy a mistake in judgment which was made innocently many years ago.

At Woodworth's suggestion the royalty clause was changed to read that the additional 5 per cent was to be paid when the annual sale reached 2,000 copies, which it did for many years.

The firm's relation with an even more eminent author, Frederick Jackson Turner, were both exceptional and typical. It began in the 1890's, when Turner became an outstanding young historian, teaching at the University of Wisconsin. His paper on the Western Frontier in 1893 had created much discussion among American historians. In February, 1895, Henry Holt and Company invited him to write a history of the United States for college classes and asked for a plan "that would appeal to the publisher's sordid soul." The idea tempted Turner. "I think the time is ripe for such a book," he replied. "But the book must not follow the old beaten path of narration, and the pathmaker's task is not to be lightly undertaken." Holt agreed and said that if Turner would let him see "a chapter or two," he would know whether or not he could offer him a contract.

A year passed. Turner had not submitted any specimen chapters, but he did write to Holt that he decided to establish his position as a scholar before he turned to textbook writing. Meantime he was in correspondence with George P. Brett of Macmillan about a volume on the Old West, agreeing to write a brief study of the Lewis and Clark Expedition. Holt wrote to him again in May, 1897, to suggest that he write the college text in three installments. This time Turner agreed. "My idea is that such a textbook should give a clear elucidation of the more important lines of development of economic life, political institutions, and social ideals." Holt sent him a contract with the normal royalty of 10 per cent and an advance of $500. Turner was satisfied and had suggested a high-school edition—when he received a more advantageous offer from Brett.

When Bristol visited Turner on October 18, 1897, he was told about the Macmillan offer and informed that Turner would sign the Holt contract if given the same royalty arrangement. Two weeks later Holt sent him a new contract embodying the improved terms and providing an advance of $1,500 payable in three parts—$500 on the delivery of each third of the manuscript. "We want it to go on record," Holt wrote, "that we have never before risked as high terms on any educational work whatever, and unless there is a revolution in business methods, we do not expect to risk them again." Later Turner also signed a contract to write a high-school text on similarly favorable terms.

The years passed. In 1903, Holt wrote to Turner, "We don't want to bother you, but venture to undertake the satisfaction of our curiosity as far as to inquire how you find yourself getting on with the High School History." Two years later, having learned that Turner had agreed to prepare an elementary text for Ginn, Holt reminded him that the high-school book came first and offered to make him a cash advance "to free you from the financial cares that interrupt." Turner accepted advances from both Holt and Ginn with the intention of writing both volumes without further delay. Yet he had nothing to show in 1908, when he wrote to his wife that he had "lunched with Bristol of Holt & Co., who is a gentleman and didn't worry me."

In 1910, Holt published THE TURNER STUDIES IN AMERICAN HISTORY, a volume of contributions by former students of Turner. The authors had agreed to buy a certain number of copies to defray the cost of publication, but some of them never did. Meantime Turner had been called to Harvard and was no further advanced on the textbooks.

Five more years passed. In 1915, the Holt firm offered to cancel the $500 advance and to give him $1,500 on completion of the college text. Eager as Turner was to write the histories and much as he was in need of money—he lived extravagantly—he simply could not get down to writing. Professor Ray Billington, who knew him intimately, commented on this blockage: "Intellectually, emotionally, and physically he was incapable of the sustained effort needed to complete a major scholarly volume." Turner knew this. To Holt he admitted, "I am not a good saga-man. My strength, or weakness, lies in interpretation, correlation, elucidation of large tendencies to bring out new points of view."

When Turner was invited to deliver the Lowell Lectures in 1917, the topic to be "The United States and Its Sections, 1830–1850," the Holt firm at last sensed something tangible and sent him a contract for their publication with a top royalty of 15 per cent of list. In May, 1918, Turner informed Bristol that eye and arterial troubles had kept him from doing any writing:

[The oculist] may be only an unnecessary alarmist about my arterial system, and I would *give* an eye for a worth-while book, or even consent with some serenity to being suddenly snuffed out, but I shouldn't wish to smoke out like a spluttering candle. . . . These admissions are unpleasant to make, but you have a right to know that my delay is not pure laziness, or dilatoriness from overscrupulous

Bristol's reply was one of shock. "The public can't afford to have
you take any chances with your sight or your arterial system. . . . Pray
don't think again about giving 'an eye for a worth-while book.' I should
say that the thing was unthinkable if you hadn't uttered the terrible
jest." The next year, with the war over, Bristol suggested a volume of
Turner's written essays. Turner replied that he had such a volume in
mind "when the time was ripe to bring them together into a revised
and fused form," but he did not think there was a sufficient demand,
and "*to use them as material for a new structure* now would somewhat confuse matters." These essays, he continued, had a certain historical value, indicating "changing conditions and older ideals and con-
ceptions, and should therefore appear in their original form." Revising
them would cause him to "lose the right to my evidence of pioneering."
He invited Bristol to be his "guest for a day or two and give me the
benefit of your judgment. I am feeling the need of a literary adviser and
'candid friend.' "

He added:

I prefer not to enter any claims, either to a "new history" or a
"new school," or anything of that sort, but to let my work stand
for what it is, and what it was at the dates when the successive contributions appeared. And above all I don't want to seem to advertise
myself. . . . I should be glad to have these essays collected and
published by you, if you can arrange copyrights, and if you think there
isn't too much of the same *motif* and too much that gives the impression of duplication.

136   Ten months elapsed before further progress was made on the contractual arrangements for the volume of essays entitled THE FRONTIER IN AMERICAN HISTORY, and several months more before the contract was signed. The long-lived success of the book is now a part of publishing history; it has been praised as a work of seminal significance and is still widely read.

In April, 1921, Turner wrote a long letter to Lincoln MacVeagh concerning the materials on sections and about the complete history of the United States. He again stated his reluctance to write narrative history and was of the opinion that his efforts at interpretation would appeal more, in general, to the graduate student than to the undergraduate.

> And finally, as I once wrote to Bristol, I have, whenever I tried to go ahead under full steam—and this is the way I write most effectively—for I must write passionately if I do it well and originally—(I am not able to sit down to so many hundred words a day as a regular accomplishment)—whenever, I say, I have tried to really *push* ahead I have landed in the hospital; and now my physical condition, though better, demands great moderation if there isn't to be a blow up of the type of Mr. Wilson's—to put a tragic event alongside my little personal drama.

He further complained that he was unable to "teach and write at the same time," and that if "retirement on a living income had materialized some years ago, I should have been in better repute with Henry Holt & Co. as a keeper of promises."

Later that month he sent the firm a check in partial payment of the $500 advanced to him in 1905. Bristol wrote at once: "I hope you will not object to my sending the note back to you, together with your 137 check, and will let this particular transaction stand as a closed incident." He again urged Turner to let Holt publish separate volumes of sections of the history. "Later we could consider a 'standard edition' of any considerable portion of the subject." Sending Turner his royalty statement the following October, Bristol again expressed the hope that he "took no offense" at the cancellation of the agreement. "I really felt that was quite fair under the circumstances. You had spent the money for assistance and got no benefit from it." Turner responded, "You need never expect me to take offense at a suggestion of yours, whatever I may think of my own duty in the matter." Yet he insisted on repaying the advance.

In May, 1923, Turner sent MacVeagh the first three chapters of THE UNITED STATES: 1830–1850, together with maps, and pointed out that he had lived with the material so long that he found the process of boiling down the details very painful; also, he wondered if, in squeezing out the details, he did not deprive the book of "the quality I should like to put into it. This may be reaction; or it may be insight!" He urged MacVeagh to be frank in his opinion of the material. "I don't want you to take it, if it doesn't seem *ready* for you—or to feel committed."

The next year Turner retired from teaching and began to work on the other chapters of the book. Illness and the unending quest for further information had kept him from completing the work eight years later when death suddenly ended his career. His friends Professors Max Farrand and Avery Craven put his manuscript materials into publishable shape. Farrand was largely responsible for the posthumous THE SIGNIFICANCE OF SECTIONS IN AMERICAN HISTORY, a companion volume of essays to THE FRONTIER IN AMERICAN HISTORY, which was awarded a Pulitzer Prize. Craven prepared the manuscript of

THE UNITED STATES: 1830–1850. Both volumes were published by Holt, the latter work being a portion of the history contracted for thirty-eight years previously.

Henry Holt and Company did not fare well financially in 1920, although its list was above average in number and quality. Its cash stringency was such that it had to stop its salesmen from traveling. One reason for the poor showing was the required large increase in its inventory, which had greatly declined during the war years. Consequently no dividends were paid in 1921. Nor did the firm have the cash to buy the shares owned by Vogelius. In explaining the reason for the delayed payments to Mrs. Vogelius, Bristol wrote: "You will realize that Mr. Holt is getting nothing whatever from the business this year and the rest of us are drawing very little." Much increased profits in subsequent years resulted in annual bonuses of 8 per cent of salary to the clerical staff and 25 per cent to all others—this largess ending in 1928, when the company underwent a change of ownership.

In 1920, the firm started a Psychic Series, Holt being seriously interested in psychic phenomena. He urged MacVeagh to import 1,000 sheets of Lord Dunraven's book on D. D. Home, a leading medium. In the same year he wrote to Kegan Paul, Trench and Trübner in England that he was eager to bring out American editions of works in this field. "From what I have told you, and possibly from other items within your knowledge, you may realize that the interest of my concern in Psychical Research is very strong, and not entirely unintelligent." The company's interest evaporated very quickly after Holt's death.

The following incident indicates how some books come into being. In February, 1922, the New York EVENING POST printed an editorial entitled "Blue Stocking Critics of America." Holt, then eighty-two, saw

in it an idea for a book. Learning from Strunsky that it was written
by Allan Nevins, Holt wrote to him:

It strikes me that it might be worth while to complete a book of
extracts from such authors, not confining, of course, to the Blue-
Stockings, but including Dickens and other males. How does that idea
strike you? . . . My idea is that such a book would have many of
the elements of a social history of the United States, and might be
read for other purposes in addition to amusement.

Nevins was interested. Holt then suggested more specifically the material he had in mind and also advised him not to use footnotes. He further
proposed that Nevins risk the chance of acceptance, telling him, "If I
don't like the book when done, my idea becomes yours, and you are
free to take it elsewhere." Again Nevins agreed, and in less than a year
he had the manuscript ready. When two readers in the Holt office
reported negatively on the book's marketability, Holt went over it himself, liked it, and wrote to Nevins that he was "instructing the office to
go ahead with you," and suggested as a title, BRITISH TRAVELERS
IN AMERICA. To the office he wrote that he wanted the book published
at his own risk and that any deficit should be charged to his personnal
account. In fact the book sold relatively well, mostly in colleges.

Feeble as Holt was physically by 1925, he remained the astute and
acidulous publisher. When Professor A. G. Keller of Yale completed
William Graham Sumner's SCIENCE OF SOCIETY, he offered the
tremendous opus to Henry Holt after it had been rejected by Ginn and
Company. Holt informed Keller that he was sending the manuscript to
the office "with a commendatory word, and I hope you and they will
get together." He could not refrain from adding: "I never have been
quite able to reconcile his [Sumner's] turning over his FOLKWAYS to

another publisher without saying anything to me about it." To Tussey, to whom he sent the manuscript, he wrote that "as Sumner took his profitable book, FOLKWAYS, to another publisher, and as this book would be nearly certain to prove unprofitable, we feel that we have done our share by publishing the biography [of Sumner], and apparently losing something substantial on it."

One of the authors who added luster to the Holt list in the 1920's was A. E. Housman, brought to the firm by MacVeagh. A SHROP-SHIRE LAD had a peculiar history. It was first published in 1896 by Kegan Paul in an edition of 500 copies printed at Housman's expense under the pseudonym of Terence Hearsay. Two years later, the printing exhausted, Housman had Grant Richards bring out a second edition. When told there might be a profit, Housman replied: "Well, if there is, then apply it to a reduction of the price of the book. I am not a poet by trade; I am a Professor of Latin. I do not wish to make profit out of my poetry. It is not my business. The Americans send me checks. I return them."

Mitchell Kennerley brought out the first American edition in 1896. McClure and Phillips published another in 1905, and Mosher issued still another later. When MacVeagh was in London in 1922, he arranged with Richards to bring out an "authorized edition" of A SHROPSHIRE LAD and to publish LAST POEMS under copyright. At that time Housman agreed to receive royalties on both volumes, which sold well.

When Housman died in 1936, additional poems were found among his belongings. Although R. H. Thornton, Holt's president, was then in London on a business trip, Ralph Pinker gave the poems not to him but to Blanche Knopf, thereby preventing Holt from having all of Housman's poetry. The following March, Katharine E. Symons, Housman's heir, informed Thornton: "I can tell you how Knopf got MORE POEMS.

Soon after the copy reached Pinker, Mrs. Knopf walked into his office
book hunting, and walked out again with MORE POEMS. Speed was
needed, but Knopf's printing was too speedy and the volume is full
of errors."

Not too long after, William Sloane, manager of the Holt trade department, arranged for the publication of Housman's COLLECTED POEMS.
Scribner graciously gave permission to reprint new poems Laurence
Housman had used in his book on his brother, but Knopf insisted on a
high fee and finally agreed to take a 5-per-cent royalty. The estate was
given an advance of $2,500 and a royalty of 15 per cent. Holt's profit on
the edition was almost nil, but the firm had the satisfaction of bringing
all of Housman's poems in a single volume to American readers. In
1959, Holt honored Housman's centenary by issuing a new edition.

Lincoln MacVeagh was of a scholarly temperament, without Harcourt's commercial flair. Nor did he have the benefit of Holt's stimula-
tion and guidance. Moreover, by 1923 Elliot and Henry Holt, Jr., were
in the trade department and were not making things easier for him. He
was not surprised when Elliot replaced him as head of the department
and he was asked to start a "marginal" division for books neither strictly
trade nor educational. Consequently, when MacVeagh had the opportunity to start his own firm, he did.

The deterioration of a long-established trade department, with a rich
and distinguished backlist, is not readily apparent. Elliot, as a publisher,
was not the son of his father. He did what he could, but that was not
quite enough. With an attractive personality and genially gregarious, he
had no particular love of books and little business acumen. His older
brother Henry, trained as an architect and with a flair for art, had too
unstable a character to be of much use. Their brother Roland, with the

firm for thirty-four years and newly married, looked forward to retiring, which he soon did. Under them the department was slowly running down.

While MacVeagh was still in charge, he sent Elliot abroad on a business trip. Young Holt soon ran into trouble with Rolland's agent. Harcourt's representative was actively competing with him for the American rights to Rolland's new 4-volume novel, THE SOUL ENCHANTED. To get the book Elliot found it necessary to give an advance of $1,500 and a royalty of 15 per cent after 5,000 copies. "It has been most difficult," he wrote to MacVeagh. "I hope you all will realize, despite the somewhat large advance, that it would have been most unwise to let Harcourt get it."

On his own after January 1, 1924, Elliot floundered in his engagingly cheerful fashion. With SWANN'S WAY having had only a modest sale, and with SODOM AND GOMORRA possibly subject to censorship questioning, he readily let Thomas Seltzer take over Proust. The Holt firm having published Thomas Mann's BASHAN AND I, a copy of the German edition of THE MAGIC MOUNTAIN was sent for consideration. It was given to the college editor, who knew German, and he read it with mounting excitement. He tempered his enthusiastic report with the information that the novel was very long and would be costly to translate and publish. Elliot was really not interested, and Bristol considered the investment too risky—thereby letting the book, and the author, go to Knopf.

Elliot did better with De la Mare. When J. B. Pinker in 1925 favored giving De la Mare's poetry as well as his prose to Knopf, Elliot strongly protested and pointed out that Holt had been publishing poetry successfully for many years while Knopf had no prominent poet on his list. Pinker yielded.

XI. Holt's Periodical Publications

Henry Holt early had the ambition to publish a periodical. In the 1870's his agency for THE FORTNIGHTLY REVIEW proved a failure. Somewhat later, having heard that James Osgood, the Boston publisher, was ready to sell the NORTH AMERICAN REVIEW, he was eager to acquire it and make Godkin its editor. Several wealthy friends agreed to help him buy it and Godkin promised to edit it gratis until it became profitable. At the last minute, however, Osgood sold the quarterly to another bidder, who offered him immediate cash. In 1882, Holt became interested in starting a new science periodical and asked his friend President Gilman of Johns Hopkins, "Who is the best American to edit a periodical like NATURE?" Nothing came of this project either.

Early in 1890, Holt decided to publish THE EDUCATIONAL REVIEW. It was his wish to make it a monthly of the highest literary and scholarly caliber that would further the best ideas and ideals among the nation's educators. Soon PUBLISHERS' WEEKLY announced: "The scope of THE EDUCATIONAL REVIEW is as broad as education itself, and subjects relating to elementary, secondary, and higher education will be given equal prominence and attention." Holt entered into the venture with much enthusiasm. He consulted the leading educators and succeeded in engaging Professor Nicholas Murray Butler as editor, and at once began to discuss with him the need of top-notch contributors for the first issue. For the opening essay he suggested President C. W. Eliot of Harvard, with President Gilman as second choice. "If you have to go to Gilman," he wrote Butler, "possibly my name may be the hair to turn the scale." The next day he told Butler that President F. A. Walker of M.I.T. might be an even better choice. "If you feel disposed to ask him for an article to lead off with (on 'The Education of the Citizen' shall it be?) I'll back you up. Let me know so that I can write him before he has said No to you."

A few days later—he wrote frequently at the time—he expressed regret that Butler could not discuss matters with him in person, as "letters are apt to seem abrupt, unreasonable and sarcastic, when nothing of the kind is intended. . . . Therefore I exhort you never to assume that any letter of mine is any of the ugly things I have said, until you get my personal assurance of the fact." He wanted to be consulted on all problems and was particularly explicit on the questions of content that might embarrass his publishing interests. "It's only mutually safe to have us agree regarding what shall be kept out." He also advised Butler on the kind of books to review—and took over that function for himself—on the type of editorials he should write, on the character of the advertisements. "Right here and now, let me pour into your ear an injunction of sovereign wisdom. Refrain, as far as possible, from deliberately contemplating making *changes in proof,* in advertising or anything else. You have no idea what it costs, or you wouldn't speak about it in the shockingly light and cheerful manner you do." He himself, he told Butler, made many alterations in the proofs of his own writing, but he was always ready to pay the cost; and he knew from experience that most authors balked at paying for their proof changes.

Once the monthly was launched, Holt began to fear that Butler might be distracted by his many other interests. He urged him to cut down on some of his administrative responsibilities at Columbia in order to do his best as editor, and persisted in his request for personal conferences. He was pleased that the REVIEW had 525 subscriptions prior to its appearance and 331 more after the first issue. When an article had to be translated, he urged that an American do the job to assure idiomatic English. He also complained about the difficulty of getting a new magazine into libraries in view of "the myriad mushroom periodicals that assail library committees."

On April 1, 1891, irritated by Butler's inability to meet with him for
conferences, Holt wrote that unless he did so, the REVIEW would be
suspended with the April issue. Butler visited him at once and their
talk brought complete harmony. On going over the galleys for the July
issue Holt was keenly disappointed in the quality of the articles. "Can't
you," he wrote to Butler, "cut down on this horrible string of twaddle
from a half to two thirds? . . . I simply *can't go on* putting my name on
such stuff. . . . The constant turning up of this sort of thing makes me
take a very despairing view of our possible sources of supply. . . . Understand, however, that I am amiable, though despairing."

The next day he expressed an afterthought: "The articles that come
to us emanate largely from pedagogues who are anxious to see themselves in print and could not get in print to save their souls except in an
'educational journal.' Nevertheless, I think we might make a satisfactory
showing . . . if you would always carry your pruning knife in your hand
and ferocity in your heart."

He returned to the subject two weeks later and ascribed the dullness
of the articles to their lack of humor. He therefore wished Butler would
convey to his contributors the need to emulate William James's "bright
treatment," in order to make their articles less dull.

In January, 1892, Holt was pleased with the proofs of the February
issue. "It is a 'corker' as you say. I shall feel 'an honest pride' in seeing
my name on it." Subscriptions and advertising had declined, however,
and Holt was discouraged. Nor did the March issue sustain the level of
the previous one, and he wrote: "I am back now pretty nearly to my
original position—that the country, or the 'profession' can't give us
enough material that I care to publish; but let us watch, pray and
wait—until waiting becomes too expensive."

Some months later an article on philosophy so annoyed Holt that he told Butler it was "a fair example of nine-tenths of what passes for philosophy viz. expansion of commonplaces into platitudes that the unlearned consider profound because they cannot find anything in them. Let me beseech you, if you can't take the article out, to cut it down to its substance which will make very little."

For the ensuing four years no correspondence exists—probably because Butler managed to call on Holt in person. The REVIEW was published regularly and limped along without too much of a deficit. Holt's interested in it slackened, though he remained attentive to its contents. Nor were he and Bristol too disappointed that very few contributors undertook to write textbooks for the firm.

In June, 1897, Holt again complained to Butler about the limited appeal of the monthly. "How long is it going to take you to see the obvious fact that the constituency for the REVIEW is too limited and too poverty-stricken to make it worth while to do anything more than furnish the best magazine that our means permit, and depend upon the appreciation of the judicious?" In October, aggravated by the "sad sad twaddle" that continued to be published in the REVIEW, he suggested that they stop paying for ordinary articles, as the academic authors would be "generally satisfied to get into print," and pay higher fees for good articles in competition with more popular magazines. Two months later he told Butler that he was spending too much time on finding out what books in philosophy and the social sciences were worth the serious attention of the REVIEW, as he was sure there were many men "who knew pretty much everything except how to make a living and would be glad to take over this task for a dollar an hour."

A libel suit in 1899 by Tammany Hall leaders against Butler and the Holt company cost Holt considerable expense as well as the temporary loss of the use of the firm's texts in the New York schools. This soured

his attitude toward the magazine, although he wrote Butler: "It doesn't
suit my grain to wish to influence the actions of the REVIEW in any
way for such considerations." Butler, sensing this, suggested that the
firm sell the monthly to him. Holt replied: "Tell me exactly what you
want to do with the REVIEW, and I will be equally candid as to how
your plan strikes me. While I'm not dead-set on keeping it, I should
feel reluctant to turn it over to another publishing house under its
present name and form." Assured by Butler that he wanted the monthly
for himself, Holt agreed to let him have it. This would make it possible,
he told him, "for you to say anything you please without having us
bear the brunt."

Butler and Charles Holt arranged the financial terms to their mutual
satisfaction. In the letter of agreement Butler wrote, "In accepting full
control and responsibility for the REVIEW, it is a pleasure to be able to
express to you the gratification which I have had in our business association during the past nine years. The strong personal friendship
which I have formed in that time for the house and for its members,
will, I trust, continue indefinitely." Holt's reply was equally cordial. After
wishing him much success, he hoped that their friendship over the years
would "increase in preciousness geometrically."

The idea of publishing a magazine was never long out of Henry Holt's
thoughts. Soon after he severed his connection with the EDUCATIONAL
REVIEW, he began mulling over the possibility of issuing another
periodical.

Late in 1903, he confided to B. E. Stevenson, "The magazine I am
thinking of is one for fiction alone, but mighty good fiction." He wanted
"to appeal only to people of some discrimination. . . . The constituency
that will demand only the really good, is so small that I don't believe
even 10 cents a month would make the thing pay, and I do not believe

that that constituency would pay more than 10 cents." This wishful thinking led nowhere.

In July, 1907, Ellery Sedgwick informed Holt that he was planning to leave McCLURE'S MAGAZINE and wanted to know if he had "lost interest in any such enterprise as that which you were good enough to discuss with me several times last summer." Holt promptly replied that his interest was keener than ever. "It is the chief subject of my daily and nightly thoughts, and I should read with great interest your most mature views on the subject, from top to bottom." Ever the cautious and calculating venturer, he added: "I may as well say that unless further enlightenment should change my views, if I should ever publish a magazine, its main pushing would be done through specimen copies and in the character of its articles, and precious little money would be spent on advertising." He also intimated that he would pay no more than $100 for an article.

Sedgwick pointed out that with HARPER'S and McCLURE'S paying $500 for an article to such men as Professors Hugo Münsterberg and Woodrow Wilson, a new periodical paying only $100 would hardly attract writers of this caliber. "My respect for Henry Holt & Co. and the attractions of the association you were good enough to suggest carried my hopes beyond my judgment. I fear I must seek my livelihood in other and less agreeable fields, but for your consideration I shall always be grateful." Holt assured him he had "no earthly objections to publishing a decent popular periodical," and invited him to lunch to discuss the project further.

Three weeks later Sedgwick sent Holt a tentative draft of the contents for the first number of the planned periodical, featuring articles by President C. W. Eliot of Harvard and John Burroughs, and suggesting two or three stories, a book review of the month, and other readable material. Holt considered the outline "hopeful" and asked, "If an only fairly respectable number could be got out for November, with the table of contents for a regular ring-tailed screamer for December, would that strike you as worth while?"

Meantime, however, Sedgwick learned that the ATLANTIC MONTHLY was available and decided to acquire it. He apologized to Holt for dropping him. "Although I am deprived of the satisfaction of working with you, I do not want to cut myself off altogether from seeing you."

Holt's yearning to publish a magazine would not leave him. He kept talking and thinking about it, the nature of his scheme changing from time to time until it became fixed as a periodical of unpopular views and ideas. In October, 1911, Paul Elmer More expressed the hope that the project would soon materialize. "I should like to see a good solid magazine in the hands of somebody who has both the means and the knowledge to make it up." Holt's response was that he would not use "the means to make it go, if you mean dollars." He wanted "to see how far a thing appealing to the appreciative classes, can get along without advertising"—which he had characterized "as by the vulgar for the vulgar on behalf of the vulgar."

Holt's first reference to THE UNPOPULAR REVIEW occurred in a letter to Frank Jewett Mather in November, 1911. Ten months later he wrote to Grant Showerman: "I cannot get out of my senile head the notion that I am going to publish THE UNPOPULAR REVIEW. The notion has been there for a long time. The amiable intention in publishing it will be to give everything Hell, though in the gentlest and most seductive manner."

In discussing the project with his associates he told them he would assume whatever financial loss it entailed. Bristol, speaking for the

150 others, objected. "All guesses as to calculation aside, I should feel hurt at your not letting us take a full share of the risks in the enterprise." The first issue of the magazine was off the press in December, 1913, edited by Holt and published by the firm. Holt explained that he expected the periodical to be "unpopular among that large majority of the public which is fond of the agreeable fallacies." The high quality of the contents was impressive. The articles, unsigned, were critical in tone and iconoclastic in attitude. Holt explained that the REVIEW was "not a forum for discussion, but a pulpit for the preaching of what we believe to be sound doctrine." In an essay entitled "The New Irrepressible Conflict" he stated that the roots of conflict lie in "ignorance and incompetence," and concluded: "The first essential is always a clear understanding. There are lies somewhere in every human conflict. Probably the most pitiful and pernicious of all lies is that all men are created equal. The only remedy is to make it true." He also included a section of his work on psychical research, a piece on simplified spelling, which he had been preaching and practicing for some years, and "En Casserole," his obiter dicta on current affairs.

Although the REVIEW was from the first Holt's personal periodical, his high reputation and persuasive appeal attracted as contributors a number of eminent scholars and writers. Among them were many of his friends—Fabian Franklin, Clayton Hamilton, Mather, More, Jordan, Showerman, and A. S. Johnson. He welcomed dissident views if the quality of the writing merited acceptance. To Walter Lippmann, for instance, he wrote: "The chance of our disagreeing I think is very good, but I open the matter because it would be a great pleasure if you were to strike some topic which would make it possible for me to have more writing as good as that which you lately displayed in your article 'Himself Again.' " Since Holt paid relatively small fees, he could not often get what he wanted. In 1914, he wrote to Harcourt: "It's hard to find the writers, and after you have found them, hard to get 'em to write what you want 'em to, and if anybody thinks that I have a life of leisure since I began this thing, he is mistaken. I was at it till four last night." Yet he was proud of the fine voluntary articles reaching him and highly pleased with the favorable reception of the magazine.

Its fine reputation notwithstanding, it failed to attract many subscribers. Holt's appeals for more readers were of little avail. Continuing to have a deficit of around $1,000 an issue, he wrote: "The editor has worked for a good many thousands less than nothing, and worked harder than he did while accumulating the thousands now used to make up the deficit."

With the July, 1919, issue the name was changed to THE UNPARTIZAN REVIEW. The deficit remaining undiminished, Holt thought of appealing to readers to share it with him. Bristol, however, urged against it. "Don't you think that some of your friends would be surprised to learn that you are not ready (or able) to back your ideas to the tune of $4000 a year? Wouldn't that seem a small loss to those who are able to hold out?" Holt heeded the advice and continued to publish the magazine for another year. In August, 1920, he wrote to Lincoln MacVeagh that Harcourt never did care for the REVIEW and asked him if the senate really wanted to keep it going. "Some of them have a feeling that the old man should be indulged in his whim, and kept going. I don't want that feeling to count, especially to the tune of $8,000 a year, and with our present capital." At the end of the year postwar inflation and his great age combined to force its suspension, thus ending the provocative product of a zealous and zestful octogenarian editor.

XII. Holt's Own Writings

The impulse to write, awakened while a student at Yale, never ceased to agitate Henry Holt's consciousness. Knowing the haphazardness of trying to live by one's pen, he had turned to publishing. "Having always had an itching for authorship," he wrote later, "I began to think of the publishing business as being near authorship." As a publisher he exercised his talents as a weaver of words in his pungent and incisive letters as well as in his acute criticisms of the writings of others. All through his career as a publisher he consorted with the eminent men of his time as a man of letters rather than of business. In the late 1880's, with his firm solidly established and with able associates to assist him in running it, he began to give part of his time and thought to writing. After Fairholt was built in Burlington, Vermont, he would do there a day's work on business matters in a few hours with the aid of a secretary and devote the remainder of the day to his own literary efforts. In this respect he differed markedly from his fellow publishers, G. H. Putnam excepted, who were businessmen without the itch to authorship.

Holt's first writing consisted of articles for THE FORUM and other magazines. "The Recoil of Piracy" appeared in the March, 1888, issue of THE FORUM. A strong antagonist of literary piracy, he argued that it "has recoiled to the serious injury of the nation which has supposed itself to profit by it." He explained in some detail how the principle of trade courtesy developed and how it functioned to prevent "ruinous competition between American publishers" and to provide the foreign author with "most of their rights"—a practice that was "simply the result of enlightened self-interest." The emergence of the piratical reprinters he blamed on the printing and paper industries.

The manufacturers of machinery set up printing-offices and binderies right and left on credit. The paper mills needed more outlets for

their excessive products, and to secure them, literally tempted ad-
venturers into piratical publishing of vast piles of cheap books, which
were largely forced into the markets at prices that not only paid no
profits, but in most cases brought on failures that left the printers and
binders in the lurch, and often the paper makers themselves.

This piratical publishing, he continued, tempting the buyer with cheap
but almost unreadable books, crowded out the well-printed works. In
addition it broke down the "courtesy" practice, the payments to foreign
authors, and, "what is of more immediate consequence to Americans, the
best reading habits of our people and, at least until a remedy comes, the
best prospects of our literature." He concluded the article by maintaining that author-publisher relations were "of such mutual confidence and
helpfulness that choosing a publisher is almost next to choosing a wife";
and that excessive routine advertising was the bane of the publishing
business. "The greatest failure in the American book trade of this
generation was probably due to wasteful advertising, as much as to any
other cause; the most enviable success, perhaps, is due, as much as to
any other thing, to skillful advertising."

An ardent advocate of international copyright, Holt was too busy with
his own work to devote much time to its furtherance. Nevertheless he
was active on committees and wrote numerous letters to friends and
officials able to act in its behalf. In a letter to A. Thorndike Rice in
1880 he stated that he was "in favor of erasing from all copyright laws
all expressions limiting them to citizens of the country where they exist,
and leaving the results to the natural operation of economic laws."

With the copyright law finally passed, he published an article on it in
the June, 1891, issue of THE FORUM, pointing out that "though it is
not one to be proud of, it is certainly gratifying to have outlived the

154 shame of having none at all. . . . The new law will inevitably drive out the worst element in the trade and put it on the old basis again, even in relation to books which may not be copyrighted." He again condemned the pirates. "They have conducted their business with the recklessness to be expected—piling into the market edition after edition of each successful foreign book, each cheaper than its predecessor, until the publishers have destroyed themselves and each other." As for the argument that the law would deprive readers of cheap books, he insisted that it was "not only dishonest but nonsensical. There are few people who cannot buy more books than they can read, and who did not buy them before they stopped buying books at all."

The magazine articles were incidental offshoots of his current thinking on contemporary events. His concentrated effort at this time was devoted to the writing of CALMIRE: MAN AND NATURE, a work of fiction which, in 1892, Macmillan published anonymously at his expense. A long work extending to nearly 700 printed pages, it dealt with the differences between Christianity and the Church, between science and religion. Spencerian thinking dominated the discussion of religion, dogma, conscience, and psychic phenomena; and the whole was graced with an engaging love story. Judged by present standards, the novel is talky and long-winded, but it was stimulating and even daring and provocative in the 1890's. The main characters talked wisely about life and human destiny in their effort "to explain man's relations to the universe and to deduce the correct principles of conducting them."

CALMIRE had, on the whole, a favorable reception. THE INDEPENDENT called it "a singularly engaging presentation of an agnostic's picture of human life." The Chicago DIAL wrote: "The author has thought long and well upon the deepest subjects. . . . He commands resources of apposite illustration and metaphor which make his expositions

simply brilliant." A sour note was sounded by the Cleveland LEADER,
which called the book "the rankest rot, ethically and artistically, ever
published." But Professor Josiah Royce, in the INTERNATIONAL
JOURNAL OF ETHICS, stated authoritatively that "the work is an
important one, wherein a genuine ethical earnestness is well joined with
a fine and manly vigor. . . . It ought to be widely read."

CALMIRE sold quite well and appeared in six editions, each with
minor emendations. In the preface to the fifth edition, still anonymous,
Holt admitted that he wanted to smuggle a little of the philosophy of
evolution "under the guise of fiction into the minds not yet given to the
subject" and that in its fictitious overlay "it was a disguised text-book
in philosophy." As late as 1910 PUBLISHERS' WEEKLY, honoring
Holt's seventieth birthday, wrote of CALMIRE: "It was not a 'big
seller,' but it attracted the attention of widening circles of thoughtful
readers for its interesting characterization, its brilliant dialogue, and
its illuminating study of the relations of a man of high philanthropy
and culture as the head of a manufacturing establishment in a New
England factory village." Holt himself, as late as 1924, wrote mock-
modestly about the book to Professor Max C. Otto: "It was a sugar-
coated chaotic philosophy. I did not write it exactly intending a novel.
God knows what I did intend. I was only a boy of sixty, or thereabouts,
at the time."

At the height of the agitation against anarchism in this country in
1894, Holt contributed an article on it to the August issue of THE
FORUM. To him anarchism was a destructive and delusive philosophy,
and he considered its leading exponents charlatans. "Freedom of speech,"
he maintained, "cannot be claimed for the anarchist as one of the rights
of freemen in times of peace; he is not a freeman, but a self-declared
outlaw, and he also himself declares that there are for him no times of

peace." As a self-proclaimed enemy of the state, he continued, the anarchist was ready to resort to any degree of violence. "The absurdity of any community harboring such an enemy needs no demonstration." He admitted, however, that anarchism was "simply one form of the widespread social discontent."

In 1905, Doubleday, Page and Company published anonymously a small volume entitled THE CONFESSIONS OF A PUBLISHER. The book created a good deal of discussion within literary and publishing circles and was soon known as the work of Walter Hines Page. Bliss Perry, then editor of ATLANTIC MONTHLY, saw the desirability of an article on the subject and asked Henry Holt, the dean of publishers, to write it. Holt agreed, and in due time wrote the longest essay ever published in that august periodical. It was featured in the November, 1905, issue under the title of "The Commercialization of Literature."

Holt and Page were generally in basic agreement. Although Holt had long liked to think of publishing as a profession, he repeatedly and reluctantly had to admit that it was in fact a business. "Yet there are features in publishing which rise to a professional dignity. . . . It may be remembered that a few publishers exercise an appreciation of literature in large superiority to financial considerations." He also concurred with Page that "an author needs a publisher with whom he shall be identified all his days," and that a literary agent had no place in this relationship.

A good book may not be an attractive one. Whether it is or not, almost anybody can tell better than the author. If it is not, a good publisher is apt to see how it can be made so; and a very good publisher, how it can be made so without prejudice to its artistic quality. But to give his best advice, he must have his heart in his work, and must know not only the book, but his man, and be in sympathy with him. This is not an affair of hours or days, but of a long intimacy, such as has occasionally adorned the records of literature and human nature.

Holt's contempt for the literary agent was even greater than Page's. When one told him that another house was offering higher terms to one of his authors, Holt replied: "The argument that another man will make a fool of himself if I don't, doesn't appeal to me." And this reproach he extended to mercenary authors and plunging publishers:

The more authors seek publishers solely with reference to what they will pay in the day's market, the more publishers bid against one another as stock brokers do, and the more they market their wares as the soulless articles of ordinary commerce are marketed, the more books tend to become soulless things.

More critical than Page of commercialized publishing, Holt assumed that Page "evidently began business when the commercializing was well under way, and therefore does not appreciate the total increase of it." His own experience was that "the literature of our mother tongue has been commercialized to an extent not dreamed of in any time of which I have any knowledge." He deeply deplored the scrambling and scuffling to obtain best-selling authors:

The mad quest for the golden seller, the mad payment to the man who has once produced it, and the mad advertising of doubtful books in the hope of creating the seller,—by pictures, dummies, big letters and other methods fit only for candy, whiskey, tobacco, and other articles of unlimited sale.

Fifteen months later Holt reiterated his criticism of commercialized publishing in an article in PUTNAM'S MONTHLY. "It would be an immense gain for the cause of literature," he concluded, "and to the profit of all worthy authors (though at the expense of the unworthy ones), if the 'commercial enterprise' that has come in from Wall Street and the energetic West, were taken out of the publishing business." Nor would this Jeremiad have been written, he intimated, "if accidents had not within the past few years so far removed the publishing business from the control of publishers into that of financiers."

This pessimistic view he expressed again in 1910, on his seventieth birthday, when he stated: "Probably the loss of very high literary quality is due to the fact that commercialism is draining off the talent into money-making pursuits; and especially to the new fashion developed by the literary agent of making authorship one of them."

The golden age to which both Page and Holt referred nostalgically surely had its share of dross, as a survey of publishing in the nineteenth century would make evident. The fact remains that while publishing must of necessity remain a business, it tends to attract a fair percentage of men who seek from it a satisfaction that money alone cannot provide.

For the last third of his life Holt was in fact as much the author as the publisher. Toward the end he valued his writings, such as they were, much more than his established success as a publisher. One of the great satisfactions of his life was his status as a member of the Authors Club. "I'm prouder of that fact than of anything, outside of the love of a few people, that ever came to me or could come to me." When he was elected its president, and re-elected, he considered it "the only external circumstance in my life worth recording." And he continued:

In my experience the impossible has happened: the lambs did really elect the wolf their shepherd, and kept him in office twice as long as they had ever kept any other shepherd, and elected a successor only when the incumbent suggested that it might be time for them to return to their traditional practice. The lambs were the Authors Club, and I was the wolf, being a publisher.

After the turn of the century he tended to give most of his time to his own work. In 1901, he arranged with George P. Brett of Macmillan to publish his TALKS ON CIVICS, delivering to him 500 bound copies and $100 for advertising. In the same year Macmillan brought out a section of the volume, "Talks on Taxation," as a pamphlet in order to take advantage of "the present agitation of the subject." Six years later an enlarged edition was published by Houghton Mifflin. In the new preface Holt stated that "in broad civic questions, the wisest man can only feel his way—as Lincoln did." The book discussed the principles of economics and social problems from the standpoint of the nineteenth-century social Darwinist, but couched in terms of ripe wisdom rather than doctrinaire strictness. The book was well received but had a small sale.

Holt's second novel, STURMSEE: MAN AND MAN, Macmillan published anonymously in 1905. It stressed the philosophy of evolution as applied to the problems of labor, suffrage, and the arts—making the point that all reform and progress must evolve out of the experience of individuals. The fictional aspects, while interestingly developed, were largely incidental. As he remarked in this connection: "I don't care to tell mere stories: largely, perhaps, for the reason that a certain famous personage did not care to eat certain grapes." The book was widely and favorably received. The DIAL termed it "a singularly ripe and balanced conception of the whole duty of man as seen in the light of the evolutionary philosophy." The LONDON ILLUSTRATED NEWS wrote: "To those who will delight in fresh and forcible thinking applied over a wide field of human relations, we warmly recommend it."

It is not clear why Holt did not publish his early books with Houghton Mifflin, a firm he had long admired. The record merely shows that when Charles Scribner declined to handle CALMIRE, Holt took it to Brett. In 1905, however, George Mifflin agreed to issue new editions of Holt's two novels and his volume on civics, with the assurance that he would treat them "with as much concern as if they were our own." At his urging Holt agreed to have the novels issued with his name on the title pages.

In announcing the new editions, Houghton Mifflin asserted: "These two brilliant novels have caused more discussion than perhaps any other anonymous work published in the last quarter of a century." Writing to Holt of the favorable review in the Boston TRANSCRIPT, Mifflin stated: "We ourselves think so highly of the books that for the moment the authorship and publishing enthusiasm become merged in the common feeling of pleasure that so prominent a notice had been made in the TRANSCRIPT." The books sold relatively well at first, but hardly enough to yield a profit to either author or publisher. When Holt suggested a new book of essays, Mifflin politely declined.

Magazine editors welcomed articles by Holt. In 1906, the OUTLOOK had him write the opening essay in a symposium on "The Creative Spirit in Literature." In October, 1908, the ATLANTIC printed his thought-provoking discussion of "Competition." On his seventieth birthday PUB-

LISHERS' WEEKLY invited him to reminisce in its pages, which he did
at some length. He stated that publishing had been more important after
the Civil War than it was in 1900, since "fortunes from other sources
have enormously advanced and men seem now to command an influence
by brute force of dollars which then was more readily conceded to
character and high tastes." He wrote glowingly of the older generation
of publishers and became acidulous toward their current successors when
referring to the Macy case.

I was not invited to attend the meeting which resulted in the foundation of the Publishers Association, possibly because I am too "im-
practical." But I have been invited to pay my share of the legal expenses and damages entailed by their policy of trying to control others
instead of agreeing to control themselves—a policy that I don't think
the fathers of any of them (so far as they had fathers in the trade)
would have fallen into.

In 1915, he wrote his vivid recollections of Godkin for the fiftieth-
anniversary issue of the NATION.

Throughout this period Holt was devoting much of his time and
thought to psychic research and the question of immortality. A skeptic
much of his life, he gradually came to reject the idea that one's life
ended with physical death. In the 1890's he investigated the claims of
mediums and studied the researches of scholars who were seeking to
penetrate the mystery of life after death. His own first work on the
subject appeared in 1914. Five years later he brought out a second
enlarged, 2-volume edition entitled THE COSMIC RELATIONS AND
IMMORTALITY. Deeply read in the literature, he dealt at length with
the various aspects of "postcarnate life" and cited evidences of psychic

phenomena. His conclusion was that there is "not only a future life, but that it is a life superior to the ills and pettiness of earth, with a morality above the reach of the earth." As might have been expected, the work was well reviewed by the serious journals but it enjoyed only a modest sale.

Holt's last published book, THE GARRULITIES OF AN OCTO-GENARIAN EDITOR, issued in 1923, a collection of reminiscences and essays which had first appeared in THE UNPARTIZAN REVIEW and other periodicals, was read widely and appreciatively. It had a front-page review in the New York TIMES "Book Review," and the INTER-NATIONAL BOOK REVIEW wrote that it was "one of the most de-lightful human documents printed on this side of the Atlantic since Franklin's AUTOBIOGRAPHY." Holt himself, writing to Professor Max C. Otto in February, 1924, commented ironically on his belated popularity: "That book, of which you speak so kindly, has had a recep-tion that has atonished me. Nothing that I had written before had any-thing like it, and of course I consider my COSMIC RELATIONS im-measurably more important."

Holt's final work, THE HOPEFUL BORDERLAND, was in galley proofs at the time of his death. It was an effort to provide thoughtful man with the "comfort that religion has not entirely assured." Sometime later Mrs. Holt took the proofs home to work on them. Although she devoted much time to the task, she died years later without completing it. The proofs, along with his vast personal correspondence, much of it with men of international eminence, disappeared in the process of family dispersion.

Henry Holt died on February 13, 1926, leaving an estate of over a million dollars. His library on psychic research was bequeathed to the Authors Club, with funds for its maintenance. Obituary notices in newspapers and magazines were long and laudatory. PUBLISHERS' WEEKLY expressed a common appraisal:

He was a man of unforgettable presence, erect and vigorous, with a deeply seamed face, shaggy brows, deep-set eyes, eyes that snapped with appreciation of the give and take of intellectual and witty discussion. No American imprint has been more markedly the shadow of a live and vigorous personality, and no figure in publishing can more completely exemplify the fine traditions that gather about the word "publisher."

The NATION noted another of his special qualities:

The chief distinction of Mr. Holt, after all, was that he was an educated publisher. There have never been many of his kind, and there are none too many now. A good publisher will be a good business man, and Henry Holt was that, but in addition he will possess a disinterested love of wisdom and good literature, will know how to talk more than gossip with his best authors, and will be capable of some degree of authorship himself.

For the next thirty months after Henry Holt's death the firm continued to operate without change of personnel or direction. The education divisions pursued their dignified and profitable activities; the trade department, headed by Elliot Holt, published a number of books every season, but few were of either notable merit or potential popularity. Two novels he had obtained while in England, Rosamund Lehmann's DUSTY ANSWER and H. W. Freeman's JOSEPH AND HIS BRETHREN, became selections of the Book-of-the-Month Club and mild best sellers, but they did not save the department from annual deficits.

Meantime the executor of the Holt estate and the family agreed to dispose of its holding in the firm. When an offer was made by R. R. Smith, Macmillan's ambitious college manager, E. N. Bristol and his associates realized that such new ownership would mean a disruption of their careers. They therefore arranged to take control of the company by means of a public issue of stock to be marketed by E. H. Rollins and Sons. Up against a shrewd bargainer and fearing competitive bidding, Bristol agreed to pay a high price for the tangible and intangible assets. "A" and "B" shares were issued; an "A" share, which was a nonvoting stock, and half of a "B" share were sold for $28, with $1.80 a year in dividends, figured cumulatively. Bristol became the majority "B" stockholder with 51 per cent, and the other major executives received proportional percentages. The transaction was concluded in November, 1928, and the two Holt sons resigned.

In the reorganization of the company Bristol retained the presidency; Horace Butler, head of the school department, became vice president; Herbert G. Bristol, then in charge of production, was elected treasurer; and R. H. Thornton, manager of the college department, was made secretary. Elliot Holt's place in the trade department was given to Herschel Brickell, the new trade editor.

Although the change of control was primarily a financial transaction, and the management of the firm continued in a low key through the depressed 1930's, the transition from family to public ownership later made possible the remarkable transformation of the company into one of the largest publishing houses in the United States. This epoch in the Holt history the present management considers too recent to treat at this time.

XIII. Holt Relations with Robert Frost

Robert Frost's connection with the Holt firm extended over forty-eight years, being not only one of the longest author-publisher relationships on record, but also one of the most noteworthy in the annals of publishing. Because he was a discovery of Mrs. Henry Holt and some of his best poems were published during Henry Holt's lifetime, but primarily because he was one of the company's most distinguished authors and intimately associated with its long history, it seemed fitting to tell the story of this relationship despite the fact that it falls largely in the period subsequent to Henry Holt's death.

William James and Robert Frost, probably the two most eminent authors published by the firm, offer a striking contrast in author-publisher relations. James's most important work was brought out by Henry Holt and the two became warm friends, yet a curious misunderstanding sent James to another publisher. Frost, on the contrary, remained with the firm despite his lack of contact with Henry Holt and notwithstanding the frequent shift of his editors and the allurements of competing publishers. And his intimacy with A. C. Edwards during the last 16 years of his life was as rare as it was mutually gratifying.

Frost came to the firm's attention while he was still sojourning in England. In 1914, when he was forty, the small English house of David Nutt brought out NORTH OF BOSTON, having issued A BOY'S WILL the year before. In his WISDOM interview in 1958, Frost explained why he was first published in England. "It was more or less an accident that it happened over there. I had never been discouraged in America, I had never been much encouraged." Both volumes were well received by English reviewers. Edward Thomas, the poet who later became Frost's close friend, wrote of A BOY'S WILL: "These poems are revolutionary because they lack the exaggeration of rhetoric. Many, if not most, of the separate lines and separate sentences are plain and in themselves nothing. But they are bound together and made elements of beauty by a calm eagerness of emotion."

Mrs. Henry Holt, who was very much interested in poetry, came upon a copy of NORTH OF BOSTON the summer it was issued and liked it so much that she urged her husband to issue an American edition. She also wrote to Frost in England to express her appreciation. Interestingly enough, Amy Lowell, who was also greatly impressed by the poems, had urged Houghton Mifflin and Macmillan to publish the book but without success. The Holt firm was interested, however, and Roland Holt wrote to Mrs. Nutt:

Mrs. Henry Holt, who is very enthusiastic over Robert Frost's NORTH OF BOSTON, has very kindly loaned us her copy. The two readers we had look at these poems found them uncommonly interesting and, while we cannot see a paying market here for this particular volume, still we are so interested in this author's work that if you have some later book of his for which you would care to offer us the American rights, we would be most happy to consider it.

Mrs. Nutt urged Holt to take sheets of NORTH OF BOSTON and offered 250 sets at a shilling a copy. Harcourt had in the meantime informed her that on further consideration the firm was willing to take 150 sheets "at a reasonable price," provided "you would assure us that we can have the refusal of the American market on the author's next book." Holt published NORTH OF BOSTON on February 20, 1915. The month before, with enthusiasm for the book on the rise, Harcourt asked permission to print the volume in the United States, but Mrs. Nutt refused. Nor was she prompt in sending the additional 200 sets of sheets for which he cabled. That March the Holt firm informed Mrs.

Nutt that, since she had not replied to the letter of the previous month,
it was forced to print the book to protect it against piracy and take
advantage of the current interest in the poems.

Meantime Frost had returned to the United States on February 22.
Almost penniless, he was very grateful for a liberal check from the
NEW REPUBLIC for one of his poems, which Harcourt handed him
on his arrival. Amy Lowell's highly laudable review in the same weekly
also pleased Frost greatly. To his friend, Sidney Cox, he wrote a few
days later: "You know that the Holts have my book out. Pretty cover.
But the best of the Holts is that they are going to be a father to me."
Many years later he remarked: "I have belonged to Henry Holt and
Company all the years since. I owe them a great deal." Agreeing with
Harcourt about the American printing, he wrote in March, 1915, that it
"might be better to bring out a small American edition than run the
risk of losing a market by wasting time over such a haggler as Mrs.
Nutt."

Harcourt was quick to perceive Frost's value as an author. Unaware
that Amy Lowell had offered NORTH OF BOSTON to two publishers,
he told Frost in July that he wanted to publicize the fact that the book
was first published in England simply because Frost happened to be
living there in 1914 and that it had not been submitted to any other
American publisher. Ten days later Harcourt wrote to Henry Holt: "I
enclose a letter from Robert Frost which Mrs. Holt will like to see.
From the attention Frost is receiving it looks as if we should thank her
for the most distinctive addition to our list this year." Two months later
he informed Holt's secretary that he had Frost visit him at home. "He
has more quality and a more lovable personality than anybody I've come
at all close to for some time, and his character and brains have deepened
my faith in his poetry. He's a 'real feller'—no mere poet!"

168 Mrs. Nutt was proving unreasonable in her insistence on keeping Frost to the terms of his contract with her. Since that would have meant submitting his next books to her alone, the Holt firm sought in vain to arrange with her for the American rights to Frost's work. Harcourt consulted with the firm's lawyers to see if Frost's contract with her could be declared invalid. At this time Frost wrote to Harcourt: "You may believe I am anxious to hear of any hope of being wrested from Mrs. Nutt. It seems to me that if I am to remain that lady's for life there will be no more poetry. What would be the use of writing just to be cheated out of royalties by her?"

The Holt lawyers pointed out that since Frost had carried out the provisions of the contract but had received neither an accounting nor royalties from Mrs. Nutt, he had a right to demand both or consider the contract void. At their suggestion Frost wrote her to this effect. Not hearing from her for several months, Frost again wrote in April, 1916: "You are hereby notified that all my obligations under my contract with you dated December 16, 1912, and also all your rights thereunder are at an end"—the wording having been supplied by the lawyers. Mrs. Nutt now replied, but still refused to release him. At the advice of the Holt lawyers he did not reply. She threatened suit, and matters dragged until her firm went bankrupt.

Meantime Frost was in financial distress. When Harcourt telegraphed him in August, 1915, to come to New York for consultation, Frost told him frankly that he had not "the money in hand to pay my fare to New York." Then after a reference to Mrs. Nutt, he continued:

I mustn't go into harrowing details, but I really have reached a pass where I must earn a little or perish. I trust you see no reasons legal moral or ethical why I should not accept that part in the success

of the book that you wanted me to have. Let me speak frankly. At
the moment when I have so much to be glad of in the general approval of my book, I am actually nearer worrying about money than
I have had to be for a number of years.

Harcourt promptly sent him a check for $200 and wrote:

We are going to take our chances with Mrs. Nutt, and pay you
what would amount to a royalty of 10% on our sales of NORTH OF
BOSTON and A BOY'S WILL in our own reprint. We expect to con-
tinue this honorarium unless we should be stopped. . . . Don't worry.
You're going to be able to publish poetry and get your just dues.
We'll go into all that when you come down. Of your troubles that
I've heard, hay-fever is the worst.

Frost's reputation was becoming firmly established. His poems were
being published in the quality magazines, and he personally was gaining
friends and admirers. In February, 1916, Dorothy Canfield Fisher wrote
to Harcourt: "I heaved a long, satisfied sigh of pleasure to know that
Mrs. Frost is as fine as her husband . . . though I'd known it ever since
I saw him. He looks like a man whose wife is as fine as he . . . that's
one of the ways he looks. . . . And isn't that simply glorious about 6000
copies of NORTH OF BOSTON and still going!" The next year another
Holt author, Carl Sandburg, wrote with equal admiration to Harcourt:
"Met Frost; about the strongest, loneliest, friendliest personality among
the poets today; I'm going to write him once a year; and feel the love
of him every day."
Early in 1916 Frost hesitated to let Holt publish a new book of his,

170 "with Mrs. Nutt hanging over me the way she undeniably is." He feared that it might cost him a good deal of money before he was rid of her. "I confess," he wrote to Harcourt, "I rather hate the prospect of having to divide all I am ever likely to earn by writing between her and the lawyers. It would put me all out of sorts—quite fundamentally out of sorts." Yet he urged Harcourt to visit him about it. "I would like it if our differences touching the next book would resolve into a sort of pow-wow or battle of wits like a horse trade in which time is no object and in which the decision goes to the best talker." At the end of the pow-wow Frost agreed to let the firm publish MOUNTAIN INTERVAL that November.

Frost's financial condition remained precarious. In December, 1916, he was invited to read his poetry at Amherst College. While there President Meiklejohn offered him a second-semester appointment as a lecturer with a salary of $1,500. Somewhat later he began receiving a monthly check of $100 from Holt in addition to his royalties—this gratuity being given for his occasional advice on a manuscript until 1921, when Frost went to the University of Michigan as a Fellow in the Creative Arts at a salary of $5,000 a year.

When Harcourt decided to form his own publishing company in 1919, he invited Frost to join him. Frost's reply was unequivocal:

There is only one answer possible to your question. I am under obligations to Henry Holt and Co. for endless favors. But so far as I am concerned you are Henry Holt and Co. You are all the Henry Holt and Co. I have known and dealt with. Where you go I naturally go. I am with you with all my heart.

I promise to do all I can to make you a great publisher even as I expect you to do all you can to make me a great author. Always yours.

On July 4, 1919, Frost again wrote to Harcourt, encouraging him
and wishing he himself were part of the new company. "I shall hope to
have a book in on one of the earliest lists of the new firm. But we *will*
try to have my affairs straightened out so that I won't have Mrs. Nutt
hanging over me, however shadowly when I next publish, won't we?"
He also told him of a prospective young author on the Amherst faculty.
"Some day presently when he's just ripe I'll send him to you."

In the light of these letters it might seem strange that Frost did not
follow other Holt authors into Harcourt's firm. Many years later Frost
explained why he remained with Holt. It was his fixed wish to have all
his books with one publisher, and Harcourt had assured him he would
arrange the transfer. When Frost visited Harcourt in the fall, he asked
him if Holt had released his books and was told that the arrangement
had been made. Frost asked to see the letter of transfer. Harcourt pre-
tended to look for it, but failed to produce it. Frost then suspected that
Harcourt was not being frank with him and decided to remain with
Holt. To Sidney Cox he wrote in January, 1920:

> At the time you wrote me about your proposed book I was hanging
> as it were between two publishers and not in a position to do anything
> for you with either. Harcourt my friend had quarreled with my friend
> Henry Holt. . . . It looks now as if I would belong to Henry Holt
> because he refuses to surrender me to Alfred Harcourt, on demand
> and representation. I'm like the lady who didn't care much either way
> so long as it was settled one way or the other.

What sweetened the situation for Frost was that Harcourt's place at
Holt was taken by Lincoln MacVeagh, a young man of classical interests
and pleasing personality. There is no clear evidence that the monthly

gratuity to Frost, started in 1917, continued without interruption. Mac-Veagh, however, paid them regularly till 1921 and gave public notice that Frost was the firm's poetry consultant. In November, 1920, Frost wrote to Professor G. R. Elliott of Amherst: "The latest interposition in my favor when I had ceased to deserve further clemency is an appoint-ment as *Consulting Editor of Henry Holt & Co.* I owe this under Heaven to Lincoln MacVeagh." On the same day he wrote to MacVeagh: "Not so much what you did as the way you did it convinces me that I have been right all along in looking for a business relationship into which friendship could enter. I like to see the opposite of cynicism in me rewarded. Of course thanks no end. And thanks to Bristol, too, if you'll convey them."

MacVeagh had Frost read a number of poetry manuscripts and re-ceived sound advice. To Ridgely Torrence, Frost wrote: "It is true I am a scout for Henry Holt. Now what I am particularly out for is left handers with something besides speed on the ball." When MacVeagh sent him Glenn Dresbach's poems, Frost suggested that Holt "go slow on him." Much as he hated to see a good book lost, he thought it had "too much of it to be good," and urged cutting. "That's what we should be here for. A lot of young writers only come to something by a reduc-tion they make themselves or others make for them." His reaction to Babette Deutsch's PORTRAITS AND PAGEANTS was much more favorable. "She can write. She has more poetic ideas than all the poets in manuscript I have read this year put together. She's a perceptible person."

In the fall of 1921 Frost went to the University of Michigan and remained in residence till the following June; again from February till June in 1923; and finally in February, 1926. His income from this fel-lowship, from royalties, from permission fees, which Holt paid in full,

from lectures, and later from his academic connection with Amherst
kept him fairly adequately provided in the years ahead. In 1922, Holt
brought out a new and more attractive edition of NORTH OF BOSTON
and arranged with Heinemann for British editions of Frost's three volumes. The following spring Holt published his SELECTED POEMS,
and in November NEW HAMPSHIRE—with royalty raised to 15 per
cent of list—the book that gave Frost his first Pulitzer Prize. Things were
going well with him and he expressed his friendship for MacVeagh in
January, 1923: "You are the only hold (or should I say holt?) the Holts
have on me I sometimes think." The following November, when Mac-
Veagh intimated that he was about to leave Holt, Frost replied: "The
only move you would have to seek my approval of before you made
it would be getting out and leaving me alone with the heirs of Henry
Holt. I'll bet that is what you're contemplating; but if I thought at all
seriously, I would come right down to New York to talk you out of it."

When MacVeagh did leave Holt at the end of 1923, Frost felt friend-
less within the firm. He had no cause for complaint, but he missed the
warm friendship and devotion Harcourt and MacVeagh had given him.
He did not know the Holt sons and later claimed he had never met
Elliot Holt. In June, 1925, he intimated to Louis Untermeyer his indeci-
sion about remaining with Holt. Referring to his next book, he said, "I
can't make up my mind about, whether to throw it to Holt, Harcourt,
MacVeagh, or Knopf." When WEST RUNNING BROOK was nearing
completion in 1927, several publishers made overtures to him. Mrs.
Frost, however, who looked after business matters, decided in Holt's
favor after R. H. Thornton had visited the Frosts and had offered an
arrangement whereby Frost would receive a monthly payment of $250
for the next five years and any additional amounts his books earned
above that sum in royalties.

When Herschel Brickell became head of the trade department at the end of 1928, he was readily accepted by Frost, but it was Thornton on whom he relied most. In 1930, Holt brought out his COLLECTED POEMS, which was awarded the Pulitzer Prize and the equally important Loines Prize of the National Institute. This volume was designed and set up by Joseph Blumenthal of Spiral Press and the limited edition was one of the handsomest books of the year. On receiving his copies, Frost wrote to Thornton:

> I want to tell you how perfect a book I think you have made for me. I wouldn't have a thing different in the make-up, whatever I might want to blot or alter in the content. . . . I tremble and am never too happy at being exposed to the public with another book. I hope this one won't be badly received. I should like to know in general, though it is better for me to shut my eyes and ears to details.

In 1930, Frost earned $3,722.57 in royalties. At that time he indicated a desire to buy more Holt stock—he having been given the first stock certificate when the firm was reorganized in 1928. Thornton informed him he could obtain 50 shares at $18 a share, and Frost agreed to buy them. E. N. Bristol advanced the money at 5 per cent interest and at the end of the year deducted the total amount from royalties.

Brickell's leaving in 1932 had no effect on Frost, since he was already on intimate terms with Thornton. His royalties that year came to $4,532.45, and even in 1933, the worst year of the depression, total royalties almost covered the $3,000 advance. In November the arrangement for the monthly payments was renewed by mutual agreement. E. N. Bristol wrote acknowledging Frost's acceptance: "May I add that I am happy you consented to continuing the arrangement through 1934. We

do ourselves a good turn by assuming all the risk, and I shall be delighted if your royalties for the year add something—a good deal—to
your income, as well as to ours." This agreement was renewed annually
until 1938.

In 1936, Holt published A FURTHER RANGE. Chosen by the Book-
of-the-Month Club, with an edition of 50,000 copies, the book yielded
Frost in excess of $7,000 as his share. The volume brought him his third
Pulitzer Prize and sold unusually well. In the same year Holt also issued
FROM SNOW TO SNOW, a handsome brief volume intended more as
a friendly gesture toward Frost admirers and collectors than as a salable
item.

For all his eminence as a poet and person, Frost was quick to take of-
fense at an unfavorable remark or at a real or imaginary slight. In a letter to John Bartlett in November, 1927, he spoke of "my Indian vin-
dictiveness" and added, "I can never seem to forgive people that scare
me within an inch of my life." This aspect of his character burst upon
Holt in 1937 with unexpected spite. The college department had arranged with an established academic critic for a collection of essays in
American literary criticism. Unfortunately this critic had previously antagonized Frost. The book had reached the plating stage and was sched-
uled for publication when Frost informed Thornton that he seriously objected to the publication of this book by Holt and would leave the firm
if it did so. Thornton was then about to complete his editorial work on
THE RECOGNITION OF ROBERT FROST, a labor of love on his
part and a gesture of good will on the part of the company. For all his
devotion to Frost, Thornton's position as president of Holt made the request that he break the contract with an author doubly difficult.

Painfully aware that Frost's objection was an ultimatum and that the
firm could not afford to lose its leading author, the Holt executives—

176 lacking the founder's ethical firmness and independence of action—abjectly submitted. The college editor, who had originally arranged for the book's publication, managed to sell the plates to a friendly publisher slightly below cost and kept the outraged critic from suing the firm by absorbing the permission fees amounting to several hundred dollars. The distressing incident was never again mentioned by either side, but some members of the firm and the critic believed that Holt had lost something precious as a consequence.

Frost's regard for the Holt management was not enhanced by this experience. Yet when his friend G. R. Elliott wrote to him in February, 1938, "Are you going to publish your next book through Holts? Don't. Holts?/ They're dolts/ In need of jolts," Frost questioned him as to why he was so critical of Holt and asked whether they had rejected a book of him. "I'll tell you this about them," he added, "their literary department is pretty nearly on the rocks. I have my doubts of their future. This is in confidence."

In that year Frost's relations with the firm became increasingly strained. Herbert Bristol, intent on undermining Thornton's position as president, urged a reduction in the monthly payments to Frost. Learning of this situation, Frost wrote to Thornton:

Make any adjustment for your comfort. I have had a feeling that my monthly check might be an embarrassment. . . . The three thousand a year was a promise of extra effort on your part to stretch the sales. I don't want it to be too much of a strain for friendship. It is necessary for me to be friends with my publishers above all things. . . . You may name $150 a month as a compromise between your fears of Mr. Herbert Bristol and your anxiety for me. Hadn't you better go the whole length for him, whatever that is. All I ask for the

present is what the books can earn and your assurance you will do 177
your best for them.

You understand me. I am saying use me in anyway to strengthen
your position.

When the sop of reducing the payments to $150 did not save Thorn-
ton's position as president, Frost was deeply disturbed. Again he thought
seriously of leaving Holt and was sorely tempted by attractive offers from
other publishers. He favored Harcourt, but hesitated to act for fear that
Holt would not release his published work. In November, 1938, he heard
from T. J. Wilson, who was temporarily acting in Thornton's place, that
Blue Ribbon Books was offering an advance of $4,000 on an inexpensive
edition of COLLECTED POEMS and advised acceptance. A fortnight
later E. N. Bristol wrote to assure him that, although the trade department was losing $30,000 that year, it would be continued under a new
manager. He added equivocally: "I don't know what passed between
you and Mr. Thornton when your monthly stipend was reduced from
$250. Your royalty earnings by and large seemed to justify the larger
sum, and we are of course ready to continue it until you would call for
a change." He concluded with the main purport of the letter, that Wilson was to visit him to arrange future terms to his entire satisfaction.

Frost remained unreconciled. To Untermeyer he wrote: "What's eat-
ing me at the moment is how to compose a tactful letter to Edward
Bristol to get a friendly release from Henry Holt & Co. I wish I could
talk with you about it." Before he had time to compose the letter he
received one from Wilson, telling him how far Holt was ready to go to
keep him.

If you will give us all your future books, whether in verse or in
prose, for publication by us, we will pay you a royalty of twenty per-

cent of the published price on all copies sold. We will also pay you henceforth a royalty of twenty percent of the published price on all copies sold of those books by you which we published prior to the present date, December 12, 1938. Furthermore, we will pay you, during the remainder of your lifetime, the sum of $300 monthly, until you consider such a payment an unfair burden to us. These monthly payments shall not be considered returnable to us under any circumstances.

Flattered by these generous terms and pleased with news of the employment of William Sloane as manager, Frost decided to remain with Holt. He was quick to develop a warm friendship with Sloane, whose classical knowledge and literary flair greatly appealed to him. He readily accepted his suggestion that Holt issue a new, enlarged edition of COLLECTED POEMS. When the attractively printed book appeared in 1939, Sloane sent Frost the following telegram: "No satisfaction could be keener than that with which we publish today your COLLECTED POEMS. *Exegisti monumentum perrenius aere* (you have erected a monument more lasting than bronze)."

Frost was deeply moved by this felicitous praise from Sloane, and wrote in reply:

> May I say through you to the firm that I have a great sense of being published? The telegram, particularly the Latin of it, gave me a thrill I had never expected to have again from being published. The book itself is here and in noble form. I see your taste and judgment in the text of both the fold-ins of the jacket. I am happy to be in your hands.

To Untermeyer he wrote: "I got a telegram partly in Latin from the Holts yesterday saying it was their pride to let me know that my latest

book was that day on the market. The Latin gave me a stir that I never
expected to have again in this world from publication."

Sloane's energetic promotion caused the 1,200 copies of the limited edition to be increased by an additional 350. The regular edition, widely publicized, sold in large numbers. In July, 1939, Frost read Sloane's THE EDGE OF RUNNING WATER and wrote to him: "I shall look up to you now as a publisher who knows writing from having written, and respect your judgment accordingly." In the same letter he explained his reluctance to recommend the work of other poets. "I have made it a resolve to be chary of my poets with my publisher, if only for the reason that poets as a rule butter no parsnips. Your friendship and mine will surely stand the strain of our disagreeing a little about one poet."

When Sloane learned in April, 1940, that a remark of his had irritated Frost, he hastened to write to Kathleen Morrison, Frost's secretary:

The house owes him a debt of gratitude for his loyalty, and I should be sorry if anything I said or did conveyed any other impression. Frankly, my feeling is that a man who has worked so well and importantly for so long as Robert has is entitled to be accepted on whatever terms are most welcome to himself, and I would hate to have any remark of mine upset him in any way.

Later that year Sloane asked Frost to help the firm celebrate its seventy-fifth anniversary by letting him publish his new poems and a volume of prose. Frost's response was warm and co-operative. "Tell me right back in your next letter what's the latest you can wait for the prose book. I, of course, want to do all I can to celebrate your (I was going to say our) seventy-fifth anniversary. . . . And don't worry about me too much. But thanks for caring."

Sloane was delighted. "It is practically too good to be true, and you are a veritable life-saver. God bless you. . . . Last Friday the directors were most emphatic in asking me whether I was sure that I had done everything for you which you would like. They all feel, as I do, that anything in our power is not too much."

His promises notwithstanding, Frost did not have either volume ready for the anniversary. Then came the Japanese attack on Pearl Harbor and the American commitment to all-out war, and the question arose whether a book of poems could be published successfully in a time of deep stress. Sloane, however, strongly favored publication, and Frost gave him the manuscript of A WITNESS TREE early in 1942. In June, Sloane told Frost that the firm had sold 10,000 copies of the volume in two months. Frost was enthusiastic:

Really ten thousand in less than two months beats everything. . . . And then these books of Louis [Untermeyer] and then my prose book, and then a volume of plays, and then another volume of poetry, and then somewhere in the middle of all this the definitive augmented NORTH OF BOSTON, should assure us of sustaining this excitement for a while yet. You were right about publishing this spring and we are glad you stuck to it—war or no war.

When the book gained Frost his fourth Pulitzer Prize, Sloane excited his rightful pride with the following comment:

This is the first opportunity I have had to write you a real note about the Pulitzer Prize. You can imagine how we all feel about it here and how glad for you we are. It seems to me that the outcome could not have been happier; you and we did nothing to try to win

the prize, but retired (so to speak) from the active lists. However, the
book was so infinitely the best of the year that even the Pulitzer Prize
judges could find no competitor—and that is that. Four times in a
single lifetime is a tremendous honor, it seems to me. [Sloane did not
know then that the judges had favored another book but were over-
ruled by the trustees.]

In 1943, Holt published COME IN AND OTHER POEMS, edited
with comments by Louis Untermeyer. The book was aimed largely at the
classroom and sold steadily, including reissues by Editions for the Armed
Services in 1944 and by Pocket Books in 1946, until it was supplanted
in 1951 by the enlarged THE ROAD NOT TAKEN. Frost's next two
books were poetical plays—A MASQUE OF REASON in 1945 and A
MASQUE OF MERCY in 1947. Of the first Sloane wrote to Mrs. Morrison: "It is loaded with dynamite from beginning to end and I don't
think that Robert has ever been more incisive, brilliant and triumphantly
wayward." Somewhat later he told Frost: "The idea of a new book from
you is always exciting to me and this present one sounds like a most remarkable thing." Sloane further endeared himself to Frost by having
Holt present him in 1945 with the du Chene bust of himself. "The great
surprise," Frost wrote to a friend, "was the Holt gift to me of the Araldo
du Chene bust I so long wanted someone who could afford it to buy in
out of neglect."

Frost underwent another wrench in his Holt relationship when Sloane
left the firm. Again without the comfort and confidence which he needed
from his publisher, and which Sloane had given him in full measure, he
now felt himself too deeply attached to the firm to heed the siren calls
of other publishers.

Fortunately for him, Alfred C. Edwards, who had recently joined

Holt as financial manager and who had neither publishing experience nor literary pretensions, offered the septuagenarian poet the admiration and advice which he now needed even more than editorial guidance. Normally Frost should have found Joseph Brandt, the firm's new president and a well-known educator and publisher, the more congenial of the two. But there was something about him that resisted Frost's confidence; whereas Edwards' simple sincerity appealed to him. Before long they developed a warm reciprocal relationship.

Denver Lindley had replaced Sloane as editor and dealt with Frost in connection with THE STEEPLE BUSH, his new book. Unlike Sloane, Lindley did not give him the devoted attention, not to mention the adulation, that Frost had come to expect. In November, 1946, Mrs. Morrison had to write to Lindley: "If your letter had not come this morning I should have called you up. Mr. Frost has been slowly disintegrating up there at Hanover perfectly sure that none of the firm like his poems." Lindley made up for the lapse by writing Frost a very appreciative letter. Two years later Frost urged Glenn Gosling, acting editor after Lindley had left, to make new plates for the edition of COMPLETE POEMS, 1949:

> You would be striking a fateful blow for me by so doing. I mean my reputation would be furthered, I'm sure, by such a mark of your belief in me. I have some repute, I suspect. I'm in no position to tell how much. . . . Many may be against me for good or bad reasons, often party-political. But there's evidence some are for me. Of these latter it would encourage me to have my publishers show themselves the foremost. Am I asking too much?

Edwards saw to it that the book was handsomely reset, and Frost expressed his appreciation in a letter in June, 1949: "It was great having that long pre-publication ride with you toward our better and better acquaintance. . . . Friends are bobbing up in every mail and calling from hundreds of miles off on the telephone to compliment me on the send off I have had from my publishers." Four months later he again wrote: "Of course K. [Mrs. Morrison] and I are glad we are going to stay with you for advice, consultation, and everything now that we have become such friends."

Shortly thereafter Mrs. Morrison assured Edwards: "You have become R F's friend. I can't tell you how much that means to him. He hasn't had one since Sloane broke out of Holt, and he's felt a bit forlorn. Now apparently you have set it right."

COMPLETE POEMS, 1949 was awarded the Limited Editions Club Gold Medal, given every three years to a work "which is judged most nearly to attain the stature of a classic." That fall Frost was also appointed Simpson Lecturer in Literature at Amherst. Just before Christmas, Edwards informed Frost, "Mr. Rigg [then president of the company] and I want to tell you how much it has meant to us to be able to publish your COMPLETE POEMS, 1949 and how delighted we are at the really wonderful reception it has had." Mrs. Morrison responded: "Many thanks for the wonderful year. It has been the best in the history of Robert's publishing."

Frost's royalties were sizable all through the 1940's, and in 1950 they exceeded $10,000. In that year Senator Robert Taft had the Senate pass a resolution honoring Frost: "Resolved, that the Senate of the United States extend him felicitations of the Nation which he has served so well."

Time helped to deepen the intimacy between Frost and Edwards. The latter devoted himself to the old poet's interests—personal, financial, and

184 literary. Although Frost was remarkably youthful for a man in his late seventies, he needed that kind of solicitous attention. In appreciation Frost made out a new will in 1951 in which Edwards replaced Sloane as "executor and trustee under this latest will." Edwards became his "banker" and confidential adviser and, as demands on the aged poet's time and energy increased, Edwards did his best to protect him from unimportant or gratuitous tasks. They saw each other frequently, and Edwards often went out of his way to accompany Frost on trips in order to ease the discomforts of travel. Frost came to depend upon him so completely and with an esteem that made the relationship rare indeed.

Frost did not publish a new book of poems for fifteen years—until IN THE CLEARING appeared in 1962. In the interval he "talked" his poems on the lecture platform, gathered honorary degrees—twenty-four of them—from leading universities, served as poetry adviser to the Library of Congress, and in general performed well as the nationally honored poet and sage. When Stanley Burnshaw joined Holt in 1958, Frost again found an editor he respected. Burnshaw had known Frost for years and, a poet himself, was in a position to take on the editorial functions in connection with Frost's writings. It was he rather than the regular trade editor who saw IN THE CLEARING through the press.

The climax to Frost's career came with his designation as Honored Poet at John F. Kennedy's Presidential Inauguration. When IN THE CLEARING appeared, it at once became a best seller. In it Frost paid homage to Edwards by dedicating to him the title poem. The poet's eighty-eighth birthday was celebrated in Washington by ceremonies at the Library of Congress, at the White House, and at a dinner party attended by the most prominent persons in the capital and by many eminent literary men. Secretary S. L. Udall and Edwards were hosts, and Chief Justice Warren, Adlai Stevenson, Justice Felix Frankfurter, and Robert Penn Warren paid homage to Frost. His response was warm, wise, witty. Nor did he forget to praise his publisher: "I have had perfect publisher relations since 1915. I have never asked for anything from them. I have never sent an accountant into the office to see whether they were cheating me, and I have grown richer and richer and they have grown richer and richer."

In its 1963 annual report, with Frost recently dead, the Holt management commented on its long and intimate relationship with him, reiterated how, when the company made its stock publicly available in 1928, it presented him with certificate No 1, and concluded: "As his sole publisher for nearly half a century, our company could not have had more distinction. Robert Frost's work will live through the ages. We shall never cease to be proud and grateful to be his publisher."

In 1964 the documentary film, ROBERT FROST: A LOVER'S QUARREL WITH THE WORLD, produced in co-operation with the Holt firm, won an Academy Award.

Outstanding Holt Books

186   The following list contains what seemed to me the important books published by the Holt firm from its early years to the present; those issued after 1928 are included to indicate the firm's continuity as a publisher of notable books.

1867	Ivan S. Turgenev, FATHERS AND SONS
1869	B. Bjornson, THE FISHER MAIDEN
	John Fiske, TOBACCO AND ALCOHOL
	Hippolyte Adolphe Taine, IDEAL IN ART
	Hippolyte Adolphe Taine, ITALY
1870	Raphael Pumpelly, ACROSS AMERICA AND ASIA
1871	Hippolyte Adolphe Taine, ART IN THE NETHERLANDS
1872	Hippolyte Adolphe Taine, HISTORY OF ENGLISH LITERATURE
	Ivan S. Turgenev, SMOKE
1873	Thomas Hardy, A PAIR OF BLUE EYES
	Thomas Hardy, UNDER THE GREENWOOD TREE
1874	Sir Henry S. Maine, ANCIENT LAW
	E. B. Tylor, PRIMITIVE CULTURE
	Thomas Hardy, DESPERATE REMEDIES
	William Graham Sumner, HISTORY OF AMERICAN CURRENCY
1876	Francis A. Walker, THE WAGES QUESTION
	Sir Henry S. Maine, VILLAGE COMMUNITIES, EAST AND WEST
1877	Lewis Henry Morgan, ANCIENT SOCIETY
	Ivan S. Turgenev, VIRGIN SOIL
	Chauncey Wright, PHILOSOPHICAL DISCUSSIONS
1878	Thomas Hardy, THE RETURN OF THE NATIVE
	E. B. Tylor, EARLY HISTORY OF MANKIND
	Francis A. Walker, MONEY
1879	John Addington Symonds, THE RENAISSANCE IN ITALY: The Fine Arts
	Simon Newcomb and E. S. Holden, ASTRONOMY (first A.S.S. book)
1880	Henry Adams, DEMOCRACY
	Thomas Hardy, THE TRUMPET MAJOR
1882	Feodor M. Dostoevsky, BURIED ALIVE
	C. A. Fyffe, HISTORY OF MODERN EUROPE
	Thomas Hardy, A LAODICEAN
	W. E. Norris, MATRIMONY
	J. A. Symond, THE RENAISSANCE IN ITALY: The Age of Despots
	J. A. Symonds, THE RENAISSANCE IN ITALY: The Revival of Learning
1883	Francis A. Walker, POLITICAL ECONOMY (A.S.S.)
	Simon Newcomb, MATHEMATICAL SERIES
1884	Carmen Sylva, PILGRIM SORROW
	Adams, Henry, ESTHER
1886	Ira Remsen, CHEMISTRY (A.S.S.)
	Thomas Hardy, TWO ON A TOWER
	Thomas Hardy, THE MAYOR OF CASTERBRIDGE

F. M. Holland, THE RISE OF INTELLECTUAL LIBERTY, 187
from Thales to Copernicus
1888   W. E. Norris, HEAPS OF MONEY
W. E. Norris, NO NEW THING
W. E. Norris, A BACHELOR'S BLUNDER
W. E. Norris, THE ROGUE
J. A. Symonds, THE RENAISSANCE IN ITALY: Italian
Literature
J. A. Symonds, THE RENAISSANCE IN ITALY: The Catholic
Reaction
1890   William James, PSYCHOLOGY
C. F. Adams and H. Adams, CHAPTERS OF ERIE AND
OTHER ESSAYS
E. W. Gosse, ON VIOL AND FLUTE (poems)
Jerome K. Jerome, THREE MEN IN A BOAT
W. E. Norris, MAJOR AND MINOR
Frances Anne Kemble, RECORDS OF A GIRLHOOD
Frances Anne Kemble, RECORDS OF A LATER LIFE
1891   Jerome K. Jerome, IDLE THOUGHTS OF AN IDLE FELLOW
Jerome K. Jerome, STAGE LAND
Jerome K. Jerome, TOLD AFTER SUPPER
Jerome K. Jerome, DIARY OF A PILGRIMAGE
Frances Anne Kemble, FURTHER RECORDS
1892   Jerome K. Jerome, ON THE STAGE—AND OFF
John Stuart Mill, DISSERTATIONS AND DISCUSSIONS,
5 Vols.
1893   Victor Duruy, HISTORY OF THE MIDDLE AGES
Victor Duruy, HISTORY OF MODERN TIMES
1894   Anthony Hope, THE PRISONER OF ZENDA (Illus. by Charles
Dana Gibson)
Jerome K. Jerome, JOHN INGERFILK AND OTHER STORIES
1895   Kuno Francke, HISTORY OF GERMAN LITERATURE
Harry Thurston Peck, HISTORY OF THE LATIN LANGUAGE
Paul Leicester Ford, THE HONORABLE PETER STIRLING
Anthony Hope, A MAN OF MARK
Anthony Hope, THE INDISCRETION OF THE DUTCHESS
Anthony Hope, THE DOLLY DIALOGUES
Anthony Hope, A CHANGE OF AIR
Anthony Hope, SPORT ROYAL
Jerome K. Jerome, STORIES, TRAGIC AND COMIC
Henry W. Nevinson, SLUM STORIES OF LONDON
H. G. Wells, THE TIME MACHINE
1896   John Buchan, SIR QUIXOTE OF THE MOORS (Buckram Series)
E. L. Voynich, THE GADFLY
1897   Kuno Francke, SOCIAL FORCES IN GERMAN LITERATURE
1898   Anthony Hope, RUPERT OF HENTZAU
Henry A. Beers, A HISTORY OF ENGLISH ROMANTICISM—
18th Century
William James, TALKS TO TEACHERS ON PSYCHOLOGY
1900   Henry A. Beers, A HISTORY OF ENGLISH ROMANTICISM—
19th Century
E. V. Lucas, THE OPEN ROAD

188

Edward Dowden, PURITAN AND ANGLICAN
George Gissing, OUR FRIEND, THE CHARLATAN
1901 Anthony Hope, FATHER STAFFORD
Karl Bucher, INDUSTRIAL REVOLUTION
Jerome K. Jerome, SKETCHES IN LAVENDER, BLUE, AND
GREEN
1903 A. Fournier, NAPOLEON THE FIRST
W. E. Norris, LORD LEONARD, THE LUCKLESS
Gabriel Tarde, THE LAWS OF IMITATION
C. M. and A. M. Williamson, THE LIGHTNING CONDUCTOR
Burton L. Stevenson's THE HOLLADAY CASE
1904 George F. Atkinson, MUSHROOMS
Herbert Quick, ALLADIN AND COMPANY
1905 Stopford Brooke, LECTURES ON SHAKESPEARE
Grazia Deladda, AFTER THE DIVORCE
Edward Everett Hale, Jr., DRAMATISTS OF TODAY
May Sinclair, THE DIVINE FIRE
Sir Donald Mackenzie Wallace, RUSSIA (new edition)
C. N. and A. M. Williamson, THE PRINCESS PASSES
1906 C. William Beebe, THE LOG OF THE SUN
E. V. Lucas, THE FRIENDLY TOWN
Burton L. Stevenson, AFFAIRS OF STATE
William F. DeMorgan, JOSEPH VANCE
Dolores Bacon, A KING'S DIVINITY
1907 L. T. Hobhouse, MORALS IN EVOLUTION
May Sinclair, SUPERSEDED
May Sinclair, AUDREY CRAVEN
A. C. Benson, MEMOIRS OF ARTHUR HAMILTON
Dorothy Canfield, GUNHILD
William F. DeMorgan, SOMEHOW GOOD
William F. DeMorgan, ALICE-FOR-SHORT
Angelo Newmann, REMINISCENCES OF RICHARD WAGNER
1908 Vernon Kellogg, DARWINISM TODAY
May Sinclair, THE HELPMATE
John Dewey and J. H. Tufts, ETHICS (A.S.S.)
Henry E. Krehbiel, CHAPTERS OF OPERA
1909 John Dewey, INFLUENCE OF DARWIN ON PHILOSOPHY
Kate Gordon, ESTHETICS
William F. DeMorgan, IT CAN NEVER HAPPEN AGAIN
1910 L. P. Jack, MAD SHEPHERDS AND OTHER HUMAN
STUDIES
Romain Rolland, JEAN CHRISTOPHE, Vol. I and Vol. II
Mary B. and C. William Beebe, OUR SEARCH FOR A
WILDERNESS
Clayton Hamilton, THE THEORY OF THE THEATRE
R. R. LaMonte and H. L. Mencken, MEN VS. THE MAN
Charles Downer Hazen, EUROPE SINCE 1815
Algernon Blackwood, THE EDUCATION OF UNCLE PAUL
1911 L. P. Jack, THE ALCHEMY OF THOUGHT
David Starr Jordan, THE STABILITY OF TRUTH
Ellen Chuchill Semple, THE INFLUENCES OF GEOGRAPHIC
ENVIRONMENT

1912 Burton E. Stevenson, THE HOME BOOK OF VERSE   189
      George Middleton, EMBERS AND OTHER ONE-ACT DRAMAS
      J. Arthur Thompson, THE BIOLOGY OF THE SEASONS
      William F. DeMorgan, BIANCA
      Rose Macaulay, THE VALLEY CAPTIVES
      Rose Macaulay, VIEWS AND VAGABONDS
      Dorothy Canfield, THE SQUIRREL CAGE
      Dorothy Canfield, A MONTESSORI MOTHER
      William F. DeMorgan, A LIKELY STORY
      Frank Jewett Mather, THE COLLECTORS
1913 Henry Lichlenberger, GERMANY AND ITS EVOLUTION IN
        MODERN TIMES
      V. G. Simkhovitch, MARXISM VS. SOCIALISM
      Julien Benda, L'ORDINATION (The Yoke of Pity)
      Laurence Housman, KING JOHN OF JINGALO
      Romain Rolland, JEAN CHRISTOPHE, Vol. III
      J. Arthur Thompson, THE WONDER OF LIFE
      C. E. Montague, THE MORNING'S WAR
1914 Martin Anderson Nexö, PELLE THE CONQUEROR, Vol. I
        and Vol. II
      William F. DeMorgan, WHEN GHOST MEETS GHOST
      Dorothy Canfield, MOTHERS AND CHILDREN
      Archibald Henderson, THE CHANGING DRAMA
      Romain Rolland, MUSICIANS OF TODAY
      Simeon Strunsky, BELSHAZZAR'S COURT
1915 Dorothy Canfield, HILLSBORO PEOPLE
      Dorothy Canfield, THE BENT TWIG
      Robert Frost, NORTH OF BOSTON
      Barrett H. Clark, BRITISH AND AMERICAN DRAMA OF
        TODAY
      William English Walling, THE SOCIALISTS AND THE WAR
      John Dewey, GERMAN PHILOSOPHY AND POLITICS
      Martin Anderson Nexö, PELLE THE CONQUEROR, Vol. III
      Lillian Wald, THE HOUSE ON HENRY STREET
      Walter Lippmann, THE STAKES OF DIPLOMACY
      Katharine Anthony, FEMINISM IN GERMANY AND
        SCANDINAVIA
      Romain Rolland, SOME MUSICIANS OF FORMER DAYS
      Edwin B. Holt, THE FREUDIAN WISH
      St. John Ervine, JANE CLEGG
1916 Sarah N. Cleghorn, THE SPINSTER
      Dorothy Canfield, THE REAL MOTIVE
      Carl Sandburg, CHICAGO POEMS
      Walter de la Mare, THE LISTENERS
      Louis Untermeyer, —AND OTHER POETS
      Arthur Edwin Krow, PLAY PRODUCTION IN AMERICA
      Richard Burton, BERNARD SHAW: The Man and the Mask
      Casper S. Yost, PATIENCE WORTH
      Sir Edward Cook, DELANE OF THE TIMES
      Kuno Francke, THE GERMAN SPIRIT
      Thomas Burke, NIGHTS IN LONDON
      Martin Anderson Nexö, PELLE THE CONQUEROR, Vol. IV

190

Robert Frost, MOUNTAIN INTERVAL
Padraic Colum, WILD EARTH AND OTHER POEMS
Romain Rolland, HANDEL
Sir Arthur Quiller-Couch, THE WORKMANSHIP OF
  SHAKESPEARE
Charles Downer Hazen, THE FRENCH REVOLUTION AND
  NAPOLEON
T. H. Morgan, THE MECHANISM OF MENDELIAN
  HEREDITY

1917 Henry Handel Richardson, THE FORTUNES OF RICHARD
  MANONEY
Dorothy Canfield, UNDERSTOOD BETSY
THE REMINISCENCES OF RAPHAEL PUMPELLY
M. J. Olgin, THE SOUL OF THE RUSSIAN REVOLUTION
Wm. M. Salter, NIETZSCHE, THE THINKER
J. Arthur Thompson, DARWINISM AND HUMAN LIFE
Lord Charnwood, ABRAHAM LINCOLN
Clayton Hamilton, PROBLEMS OF THE PLAYWRIGHT
Walter de la Mare, PEACOCK PIE
Stuart P. Sherman, ON CONTEMPORARY LITERATURE

1918 Leon Trotsky's OUR REVOLUTION
William F. DeMorgan, THE OLD MADHOUSE
Ramsay Muir, NATIONAL SELF-GOVERNMENT
Dorothy Canfield, HOME FIRES IN FRANCE
Dorothy Canfield, THE DAY OF GLORY
Carl Sandburg, CORNHUSKERS
William Beebe, JUNGLE PEACE

1919 Romer Wilson, MARTIN SCHULER
Thomas Burke, OUT AND ABOUT LONDON
Louis Untermeyer, THE NEW ERA IN AMERICAN POETRY
John Crowe Ransom, POEMS ABOUT GOD
Bertrand Russell, PROPOSED ROADS TO FREEDOM
J. Arthur Thomson, THE SECRETS OF ANIMAL LIFE
E. T. Raymond, UNCENSORED CELEBRITIES
J. A. Hobson, RICHARD COBDEN
G. Grant Robertson, BISMARCK
Romain Rolland, COLAS BREUGNON
H. J. Mackinder, DEMOCRATIC IDEALS AND REALITY

1920 Maurice Hewlett, THE LIGHT HEART
Martin Anderson Nexö, DITTE: GIRL ALIVE
Lew Sarett, MANY, MANY MOONS
Benedetto Croce, SHAKESPEARE, ARIOSTO, AND CORNEILLE
J. Arthur Thomson, THE SYSTEM OF ANIMATE NATURE
Henri Bergson, MIND ENERGY
John Dewey, RECONSTRUCTION IN PHILOSOPHY
William F. DeMorgan, THE OLD MAN'S YOUTH
William F. DeMorgan, THE YOUNG MAN'S OLD AGE
Stephen Vincent Benét, HEAVENS AND EARTH
Albert Einstein, RELATIVITY
Frederick Jackson Turner, THE FRONTIER IN AMERICAN
  HISTORY
Preserved Smith, THE AGE OF THE REFORMATION

1921 Romain Rolland, CLERAMBAULT
      J. Arthur Thomson, THE CONTROL OF LIFE
      G. B. Adams, CONSTITUTIONAL HISTORY OF ENGLAND
      William Beebe, THE EDGE OF THE JUNGLE
      Stephen Vincent Benét, THE BEGINNING OF WISDOM
      Martin Anderson Nexö, DITTE: DAUGHTER OF MAN
      Robert Benchley, OF ALL THINGS!
      L. T. Hobhouse, THE RATIONAL GOOD
      John Dewey, HUMAN NATURE AND CONDUCT
      Benedetto Croce, THE POETRY OF DANTE
      Robert S. Woodworth, PSYCHOLOGY
      Walter de la Mare, NEW POEMS
1922 A.M.W. Stirling, WILLIAM DE MORGAN AND HIS WIFE
      Romain Rolland, PIERRE AND LUCE
      Martin Anderson Nexö, DITTE: TOWARD THE STARS
      Carl Spitteler, TWO LITTLE MISOGYNISTS
      Frederic Harrison, NOVISSIMA VERBA
      Walter de la Mare, THE VEIL AND OTHER POEMS
      A. E. Housman, A SHROPSHIRE LAD (Authorized Edition)
      L. T. Hobhouse, THE ELEMENTS OF SOCIAL JUSTICE
      Marcel Proust, SWANN'S WAY
      Frank Jewett Mather, HISTORY OF ITALIAN PAINTING
1923 A. E. Housman, LAST POEMS
      George Stirling, SELECTED POEMS
      Tenney Frank, A HISTORY OF ROME
      Stephen Vincent Benét, JEAN HUGUENOT
      Thomas Mann, BASHAN AND I
      Robert Frost, NEW HAMPSHIRE
      Francesco Nitti, THE DECADENCE OF EUROPE
1924 Mrs. John King Van Rensselaer, THE SOCIAL LADDER
      Rosita Forbes, THE SULTAN OF THE MOUNTAINS, The
        Life Story of Raisuli
      AMERICAN SOCIAL HISTORY, As Recorded by British
        Travelers, Ed. by Allan Nevins
      Edmond Rostand, CYRANO DE BERGERAC, Trans. by
        Brian Hooker
      William Stern, THE PSYCHOLOGY OF EARLY CHILDHOOD
        (Trans. by Anna Barwell)
      Frederick H. Koch, CAROLINA FOLK PLAYS
1925 Romain Rolland, ANNETTE AND SYLVIE, Vol. I of THE
        SOUL ENCHANTED
      Romain Rolland, SUMMER, Vol. II of THE SOUL
        ENCHANTED
      Maximilian Harden, I MEET MY CONTEMPORARIES
      Robert Benchley, PLUCK AND LUCK
      Burton E. Stevenson, THE HOME BOOK OF MODERN VERSE
1926 Frank Jewett Mather, MODERN PAINTING: 1664–1914
      Robert Benchley, LOVE CONQUERS ALL
      Edith Sitwell, POETRY AND CRITICISM
      Romain Rolland, THE GAME OF LOVE AND DEATH
      W. A. Locy, THE GROWTH OF BIOLOGY

P. Vidal de la Blache, PRINCIPLES OF HUMAN
GEOGRAPHY
C. Lloyd Morgan, LIFE, MIND, AND SPIRIT
Ivan Bunin, MITYA'S LOVE
Alfred Noyes, THE NEW WORLD
John M. Manly, SOME NEW LIGHT ON CHAUCER

1927 Romain Rolland, MOTHER AND SON, Vol. III of THE SOUL
ENCHANTED
Alfred Noyes, NEW ESSAYS AND AMERICAN IMPRESSIONS
Robert Benchley, THE EARLY WORM
L. White Busbey, UNCLE JOE CANNON
Rosamond Lehmann, DUSTY ANSWER
John Dewey, THE PUBLIC AND ITS PROBLEMS
Harold Laski, COMMUNISM
Gaetano Salvemini, THE FASCIST DICTATORSHIP IN ITALY,
Vol. I
J. C. Squire, CONTEMPORARY AMERICAN AUTHORS
Walter de la Mare, STUFF AND NONSENSE

1928 Paul Morand, THE LIVING BUDDHA
Robert Frost, WEST-RUNNING BROOK
Gaetano Salvemini, THE FASCIST DICTATORSHIP IN ITALY,
Vol. II
Anatole France, RABELAIS
Hendrik Willem Van Loon, PETER STUYVESANT AND HIS
TIMES
THE SACCO-VANZETTI CASE—6 volumes
Robert Benchley, 20,000 LEAGUES UNDER THE SEA OR
DAVID COPPERFIELD

1929 H. E. Freeman, JOSEPH AND HIS BRETHREN
John Dewey, CHARACTERS AND EVENTS, ed. by Joseph
Ratner
Herbert Read, ENGLISH PROSE STYLE
R. A. Scott-James, THE MAKING OF LITERATURE
Ramon del Valle-Inclan, THE TYRANT
Herman Hesse, STEPPENWOLF
Forest Reid, WALTER DE LA MARE

1930 Ernest Mérimée, A HISTORY OF SPANISH LITERATURE
Rosamond Lehmann, A NOTE IN MUSIC
Preserved Smith, A HISTORY OF MODERN CULTURE:
1543–1687

1931 Edwin B. Holt, ANIMAL DRIVE AND THE LEARNING
PROCESS
Sir Flinders Petrie, SEVENTY YEARS IN ARCHAEOLOGY
John Drinkwater, INHERITANCE
Regis Michaud, WILLIAM JAMES
Albert Schweitzer, THE MYSTICISM OF PAUL THE APOSTLE
Ellen C. Semple, THE GEOGRAPHY OF THE
MEDITERRANEAN REGION

1932 Heinrich Wölfflin, PRINCIPLES OF ART HISTORY
Charles D. Hazen, THE FRENCH REVOLUTION, 2 Volumes
Paul Tillich, THE RELIGIOUS SITUATION

1933 Frederick J. Turner, THE SIGNIFICANCE OF SECTIONS IN 193
     AMERICAN HISTORY
     Albert Schweitzer, OUT OF MY LIFE AND THOUGHT
     Mary Ellen Chase, A GOODLY HERITAGE
     Stephen Gwynn, JONATHAN SWIFT AND HIS TIMES
     John M. Murry, REMINISCENCES OF D. H. LAWRENCE
1934 K. Jaspers, MAN IN THE MODERN AGE
     Romain Rolland, THE DEATH OF A WORLD, Vol. IV of THE
     SOUL ENCHANTED
     Romain Rolland, A WORLD IN BIRTH, Vol. V of THE SOUL
     ENCHANTED
     Helen Waddell, PETER ABELARD
     Preserved Smith, A HISTORY OF MODERN CULTURE:
     1687–1776
     James H. Tufts, AMERICA'S SOCIAL MORALITY
1935 Henri Bergson, THE TWO SOURCES OF MORALITY AND
     RELIGION
     Frederick J. Turner, THE UNITED STATES: 1830–1850
     Anna Louise Strong, I CHANGE WORLDS
     Herman Finer, MUSSOLINI'S ITALY
1936 Charles B. Davenport, HOW WE CAME BY OUR BODIES
     Robert Frost, A FURTHER RANGE
     Conyers Read, THE TUDORS
     Albert Schweitzer, INDIAN THOUGHT AND ITS
     DEVELOPMENT
     Howard Mumford Jones, HARP THAT ONCE—: A Life of
     Thomas Moore
1937 Mark Van Doren, THE LAST LOOK AND OTHER POEMS
1938 George Duhamel, THE PASQUIER CHRONICLES
     George R. Stewart, EAST OF THE GIANTS
     John Dewey, LOGIC: THE THEORY OF INQUIRY
     Walter de la Mare, MEMORY AND OTHER POEMS
1939 Christopher Smart, REJOICE IN THE LAMB
     Mark Van Doren, SHAKESPEARE
     Frank Jewett Mather, WESTERN EUROPEAN PAINTERS OF
     THE RENAISSANCE
1940 George Duhamel, CECILE PASQUIER
     THE COLLECTED POEMS OF A. E. HOUSMAN
     John Ciardi, HOMEWARD TO AMERICA
     Oscar Ameringer, IF YOU DON'T WEAKEN
1941 THE COLLECTED POEMS OF WALTER DE LA MARE
     Mark Van Doren, THE MAYFIELD DEER
     THE COLLECTED POEMS OF LEW SARETT
1942 Robert Frost, A WITNESS TREE
     LeGrand Cannon, LOOK TO THE MOUNTAIN
     Robert Trumbull, THE RAFT
     Marion Hargrove, SEE HERE, PRIVATE HARGROVE
1943 Ernie Pyle, HERE IS YOUR WAR
1944 Mark Van Doren, THE SEVEN SLEEPERS
     E. E. Cummings, I x I
     Joseph Wood Krutch, SAMUEL JOHNSON
     Morris R. Cohen, A PREFACE TO LOGIC

194   **1946**   Francois Mauriac, WOMAN OF THE PHARISEES
Walter Johnson, SELECTED LETTERS OF WILLIAM ALLEN
     WHITE: 1899–1943
Mark Schorer, WILLIAM BLAKE
E. E. Cummings, SANTA CLAUS: A Morality
Hilaire Belloc, THE SERVILE STATE

1947   Robert Frost, STEEPLE BUSH
Walter Johnson, WILLIAM ALLEN WHITE'S AMERICA
Herbert Read, THE INNOCENT EYE
Francois Mauriac, THERESE

1948   Herman Hesse, DEMIAN
L. L. Whyte, THE NEXT DEVELOPMENT IN MAN
Daniel Boorstin, THE LOST WORLD OF THOMAS
     JEFFERSON
Francois Mauriac, THE UNKNOWN SEA

1949   Morris R. Cohen, STUDIES IN PHILOSOPHY AND SCIENCE
Morris R. Cohen, THE FAITH OF A LIBERAL
George Duhamel, SUZANNE AND JOSEPH

1951   Omar Bradley, A SOLDIER'S STORY
Carleton S. Coon, CARAVAN: THE STORY OF THE MIDDLE
     EAST
Babette Deutsch, POETRY IN OUR TIME

1955   George A. Haven, THE AGES OF IDEAS
Walter Lord, A NIGHT TO REMEMBER

1957   Bernard Baruch, MY OWN STORY
1960   Bernard Baruch, THE PUBLIC YEARS
Stanley Burnshaw, Dudley Fitts, Henri Pegre, and J. F. Nims,
     THE POEM ITSELF

1961   Robert Ruark, THE OLD MAN'S BOY GROWS OLDER
1962   Karl Barth, EVANGELICAL THEOLOGY
Robert Frost, IN THE CLEARING
Joanne Greenberg, THE KING'S PERSONS

1963   Peter Blake, GOD'S OWN JUNKYARD
David Ben-Gurion, ISRAEL: YEARS OF CHALLENGE
Stewart L. Udall, THE QUIET CRISIS

1964   Martin Buber, DANIEL: DIALOGUES ON REALIZATION
Lawrance Thompson, SELECTED LETTERS OF ROBERT
     FROST
PRIEST AND WORKER: THE AUTOBIOGRAPHY OF
     HENRI PERRIN

1965   Christina Stead, THE MAN WHO LOVED CHILDREN
Albert Schweitzer, THE TEACHING OF REVERENCE FOR
     LIFE
Sacheverell Sitwell, MONKS, NUNS AND MONASTERIES

Index

Adams, Henry, 38f.
Advances to authors, 96f.
American Nature Series, 106f.
American Science Series, 15f.
Atlantic Monthly, 157
Authors Club, 159

Baker, George, 81
Benchley, Robert, 131
Benét, Stephen Vincent, 131
Bennett, Arnold, 114
Bentley, George, 26, 85f.
Bergson, Henri, 118
Blumenthal, Joseph, 175
Brace, Donald, 112
Brandt, Joseph, 183
Brett, George P., 133, 160
Brickell, Herschel, 175
Bristol, Edward N., 68, 100f., 113, 125f., 135f., 151, 165, 175, 178
Bristol, Herbert, 130, 177
Burnett, Arthur W., 68
Burnshaw, Stanley, 185
Butler, Nicholas Murray, 144f.
Butterworth, Thornton, 117

Calmire (Holt), 155
Claflin (H.B.), Co., 93
Commercialized publishing, 158f.
Confessions of a Publisher, The (Page), 157f.
Conway, Eustace, 85
Conway, Moncure, 73, 84f.
Cosmic Relations and Immortality, The (Holt), 162f.
"Courtesy of the trade" principle, 21f.
Cox, Sidney, 172

De Morgan, William, 104f.
Dent, J. M., 106
Doubleday, F. N., 77

Educational Review, The, 144f.
Edwards, Alfred C., 183f.
Elliott, G. R., 177
Everyman's Library, 106, 115

Fairholt, 68
Fisher, Dorothy Canfield, 119f., 170
Fiske, John, 44
Ford, Paul Leicester, 79f.
Fortnightly Review, The, 84
Forum, The, 153f.
Frontier in American History, The (Turner), 137
Frost, Robert, 124, 166ff.
Gadfly, The (Voynich), 76
Garrulities of an Octogenerian Editor, The (Holt), 163
Gehrs, August H., 113
Gilman, Daniel Coit, 5, 19
Godkin, E. L., 10, 18
Gosling, Glenn, 183
Gregor, Leigh R., 65

Hackett, E. Byrne, 129
Hackett, F. S., 99
Harcourt, Alfred, 112ff., 123ff., 167f.
Hardy, Thomas, 32f.
Harper, Joseph W., 33f.
Harper & Brothers, 86, 93
Heinemann, William, 88, 114
Holden, E. L., 18
Holt, Elliot, 129, 142f.
Holt, Florence, 167

196   Holt, Henry, education of, 3; marriage of, 4, 68; joins F. Leypoldt, 6f.; as foreign-language publisher, 8; influenced by H. Spencer, 10; on piracy, 25f., 153f.; as editor, 28f.; as publisher, 31f.; and T. Hardy, 32f.; and W. E. Norris, 34f.; and L. H. Morgan, 35f.; and J. A. Symonds, 37; and H. Adams, 38f.; and W. James, 44f.; and A. P. Watt, 69, 71, 73, 92; and J. K. Jerome, 69f.; and A. Waugh, 71f., 76f., 87f.; and A. Hope, 71f.; and Mrs. E. L. Voynich, 75f., and P. L. Ford, 79f.; and English agents, 84f.; and M. Conway, 84; and G. Bentley, 85; on advances, 96f.; and H. G. Wells, 103f.; and W. De Morgan, 104f.; and J. M. Dent, 106; and E. G. Stevenson, 108f.; and G. Showerman, 110; and F. J. Mather, 110f.; and A. Harcourt, 112ff.; and H. Bergson, 118; and D. C. Fisher, 119f.; and S. P. Sherman, 121f.; and J. Spingarn, 122; and B. Russell, 123; and A. Nevins, 140; and The Educational Review, 144f.; and E. Sedgwick, 149f.; and The Unpopular Review, 150f.; as author, 153f.; on literary agents, 158; on commercialized publishing, 158f.; and Authors Club, 159f.

Holt, Roland, 68, 117, 126, 128, 129, 130

Home Book of Verse, The, 108f.

Honorable Peter Stirling, The (Ford), 79f.

Hope, Anthony, 72f.

Housman, A. E., 141f.

James, Henry, 66

James, William, 44ff., 166

Jean Christophe (Rolland), 114

Jerome, Jerome K., 69f.

Joseph Vance (De Morgan), 104

Keller, A. G., 140

King, Clarence, 40

Knopf, Blanche, 141

Leisure Hour Series, 14f.

Leisure Moment Series, 15

Lewis, Sinclair, 126f.

Leypoldt, Frederick, 5f.

Lightning Conductor, The (Williamsons), 102

Lindley, Denver, 183

Literary agents, 69, 71, 73, 92, 109, 157

Lodge, Henry Cabot, 43

Loring, A. K., 24

Lowell, Amy, 168

Macmillan, Frederick, 11

MacVeagh, Lincoln, 129f., 137f., 141, 142f., 172f.

Main Street (Lewis), 128

Makers of the Nineteenth Century, 120f.

Man with the Broken Ear, The (About), 4

Martin, H. Newell, 19

Mather, Frank Jewett, 110f.

Meiklejohn, Alexander, 171

Melcher, Fred G., 104, 125

Mifflin, George, 161

Mill, John Stuart, 12

Miller, Alice Duer, 110

More, Paul Elmer, 150

Morgan, Lewis H., 35f.

Morrison, Kathleen, 180, 183

Nation, The, 164

Nevins, Allan, 140

Newcomb, Simon, 18
Norris, W. E., 34f.
North of Boston (Frost), 166f.
Nutt, Mrs. David, 167f.

Osgood, James R., 24, 144
Otto, Max C., 156

Packard, A. S., 28f.
Page, Walter Hines, 157f.
People's University Library, 114f.
Pinker, Ralph, 141
Pirated publishing, 25f., 153f.
Principles of Psychology (James), 48f.
Prisoner of Zenda, The (Hope), 72f.
Psychology (Woodworth), 132
Publishers' Weekly, 9, 12, 116, 125, 156, 162, 164
Putnam, George Haven, 4
Putnam, George Palmer, 4, 5, 22
Putnam's Monthly, 159

Reynolds, Paul, 109
Robinson, A. M., 80
Roosevelt, Franklin D., 130
Rupert of Hentzau (Hope), 74f.
Russell, Bertrand, 123, 131
Russell, George E., 111

Sedgwick, Ellery, 149f.
"Senate" (Holt), 117
Sherman, Stuart P., 121f.
Showerman, Grant, 110, 150
Sloane, William, 142, 179f.
Sloane, William M., 99
Smith, R. R., 165
Spingarn, Joel, 122

Stevenson, B. E., 108f.
Sturmsee (Holt), 160f.
Subscription books, 13
Sumner, William Graham, 10, 140f.
Symonds, John Addington, 37

Taft, Robert, 184
Taine, Hippolyte A., 11
Talks on Civics (Holt), 160
Talks to Teachers on Psychology (James), 56ff.
Thomas, Edward, 166
Thornton, R. H., 141, 174f.
Three Men in a Boat (Jerome), 70
Turner, Frederick Jackson, 133f.
Tussey, Moore C., 130

Udall, S. L., 186
Unpartizan Review, The, 152f.
Unpopular Review, The, 150f.
University Club, 67
Untermeyer, Louis, 128, 174
Unwin, Stanley, 131

Vogelius, Joseph, 21f., 68, 129
Voynich, Mrs. E. L., 75f.

Walker, Francis A., 19
Watson, John B., 100
Watt, A. P., 69, 71, 73, 92
Waugh, Arthur, 71f., 76f., 87f.
Wells, H. G., 103f.
Williams, Ralph O., 9
Williams and Norgate, 115f.
Wilson, T. J., 178
Wister, Owen, 105
Woodworth, Robert S., 132f.

Youmans, E. L., 15